W0112432

# BUSINESS CASE STUDIES

*General Editors:* R. G. BURNS and K. MIDGLEY

The object of the series is to enable students to gain experience in analysing actual business problems and making the decisions necessary to solve these problems.

The student is, of course, keen to become skilled at solving both actual business problems and examination problems and another of the objects of this series of books is to demonstrate that case studies provide a positive link between business problems and examination problems.

Each book consists, firstly, of case studies which either reproduce actual business problems or closely resemble them and, secondly, of a selection of examination problems which students should be able to answer more readily after having studied and discussed the case studies.

After each case study, there is a series of problems designed both to test students' understanding of the facts contained in the case study and to provide the opportunity for solving actual business problems. All the questions set have guidelines to solutions provided. The guidelines are not complete answers but more in the nature of clues as to the means of arriving at answers and starting-points for calculations thereto. The guidelines will be particularly useful for students who are studying without the benefit and stimulation provided by the frequent sharing of ideas in group discussion.

Where appropriate, brief comments on examination questions are also provided.

The earlier volumes in the series give most emphasis to the main business function which is being considered in the volume, e.g. finance, marketing, personnel, etc. Complementary functions are discussed in less detail. Later in the series there is a change of case-form to multi-subject cases, and the emphasis is then on the integrated nature of business activities.

For titles of other volumes in the series see p. 2.

# BUSINESS CASE STUDIES

*Edited by* R. G. BURNS *and* K. MIDGLEY

# Case Studies in Business Data Processing

F. W. PURCHALL
F.C.C.A., M.I.O.M., A.M.B.I.M.

and

RAYMOND S. WALKER
F.C.I.I., A.C.I.S., M.B.C.S.

Palgrave Macmillan

*First published 1972 by*
THE MACMILLAN PRESS LTD
*London and Basingstoke*
*Associated companies in New York Toronto*
*Dublin Melbourne Johannesburg and Madras*

SBN 333 13250 5

ISBN 978-0-333-13250-0

ISBN 978-1-349-01368-5 (eBook)
DOI 10.1007/978-1-349-01368-5

# Introduction to the Series

The case-study method of teaching has become increasingly popular over the last decade, particularly in the field of management education. It is a method which incorporates several of the tenets of sound educational theory: it aims to build up understanding on a framework of experience, to encourage learning by doing, and to promote interest and enthusiasm by requiring the student to solve problems in realistic situations. Case studies may be the subject of group study or may be tackled by individuals: dramatised situations may be employed and case studies may incorporate the use of documents and visual and audio aids.

Unfortunately there is still a comparative shortage of published case studies in this country; and, in particular, students on the fringe of management studies and those without access to college courses may rarely have the opportunity to work through case studies.

This series not only aims to expand the number of studies available for use on courses in colleges and universities, but also to make available case studies which can be used by students in private study.

There is no unanimity among educationists as to the nature and format of case studies. Is it essential that cases be written about real situations? Should solutions be provided for the problems set? The criterion which we have applied is that the cases should be presented in such a way as to ensure that the student has the maximum opportunity and incentive to learn by analysing situations and making decisions, where appropriate. In most instances, in order to ensure the verisimilitude of the cases, real situations form the bases of the studies. As for solutions, while we feel that it can be discouraging for students if no answers to problems are provided, we must take account of the fact that there is frequently more than one solution to a problem. Consequently, we offer guidelines rather than solutions to cases, though clearly some problems call for more incontrovertible and accurate treatment than others.

While it is our hope that this series will prepare the student for dealing with real-life situations in business and administration, we are aware that he is naturally and rightly concerned to prepare himself to cope with examinations. In fact many examination questions take the form of miniature case studies: circumstances are set out briefly, and a solution to a problem is required. This may not always be so – some examination questions simply call for information – but nevertheless, in that case studies can enrich the understanding of a subject, they can play an important role in the preparation for examination hurdles. For these reasons examination questions are set out at the end of each book, and though they are not always exactly related to the case studies therein, there is sufficient in common to ensure that each booklet taken as a whole, with case studies, guidelines, examination questions and comments, provides a valuable and stimulating supplement to the reading set out in the bibliographies which are also provided.

R. G. B.
K. M.

# Contents

# Preface

The case studies in this book have been designed to provide students of E.D.P., at undergraduate and H.N.D. level, with some practical work in the design of data-processing systems. The case studies have deliberately avoided the use of advanced techniques of both hardware and software, so that the student is compelled to face up to the problems of input, sorting, processing and output. It is intended that the student should work through each case study to provide his own solution, and only then to compare this with the guidelines and suggested solution. Failure to adopt this approach will largely negate the desired result.

Although the case studies have been prepared for students taking sandwich and full-time advanced courses of further education, the book should also prove useful for in-service and short revision courses.

We should like to acknowledge the assistance of I.C.L. in the design of the input document in the case study on Production Scheduling.

F. W. PURCHALL
RAYMOND S. WALKER

*Disclaimer*
All the case studies are fictional, and any resemblance to individuals, companies or company systems is purely coincidental.

# 1 Human Factors

*A case study by F. W. Purchall*

# CASE STUDY

Whirlwind Holidays Ltd is a company providing the services of travel agents and tour operators, specialising in coach tours. One of their most popular tours is a two-week coach tour visiting fourteen countries. The company has a turnover of around £4 million and operates through agents as well as head office and the three branches.

At the Board meeting in September 1970 John Fane, the assistant to the Managing Director, produced a proposal for placing the accounting system on a computer, using for this purpose a local bureau. The proposal outlined the present system, which was dependent on the operation of two keyboard accounting machines, and went on to describe the new system in the following terms: 'The old system will not be changed, all that will happen is that the source documents will be taken around to the bureau by hand. The bureau will punch up cards and return the documents within twenty-four hours.' The proposal concluded with a comparison of the costs of the present and proposed systems as follows:

| | | |
|---|---|---|
| Present system – 2 operators | | £2,000 p.a. |
| New system – System design, programming, testing, implementation, purchase of file media | | £ 400 |
| Data preparation | | £ 500 |
| Processing and print-outs | | £ 900 |
| | | £1,400 p.a. |

The Board were interested and asked for details of volumes. John Fane informed them that he proposed to put two ledgers on the computer. The Clients' ledger consisted of 10,000

10

accounts, the number of postings to each account averaging 4 (2 debit, 2 credit), and the Agents' ledger 1,000 accounts, average postings per account being 5. When the Board proposed postponing their decision until a later meeting, they were informed by the Managing Director that a decision must be taken at once (a) because the existing accounting machines could not be converted for decimalisation, and would therefore have to be replaced should the computer project not be accepted, and (b) there would not be time to implement the computer system by February unless the go-ahead was given at once. Accordingly, somewhat reluctantly, the decision was taken to proceed.

Some weeks later one of the directors decided to pay a visit to the accounts department. Unfortunately the company was temporarily without an accountant, but he had a long talk with Frank Page, the supervisor in charge. He found that Frank and John Fane were working closely together on the project, but that none of the other nine clerks in the department had been consulted. In fact the whole project was a closely guarded secret.

This aspect worried the director, who took the opportunity of raising the matter with John Fane at the next Board meeting. John replied as follows: 'If the new system became general knowledge, the two machine operators, Joan and Sylvia, would leave and get another job, because it would be obvious to them that after February their jobs would disappear.'

Just after Christmas, three accounts clerks, whose jobs would not have been affected by the new system, handed in their notice and left. About the same time a director, making a routine visit to the branches, discovered from Bill Travers, one of the branch managers, that the staff in the branches were very concerned that the computer would increase their work-load, a very important factor, as they were about to enter their busiest period. He decided to make a quick check and discovered that, although some forms had been redesigned, and one form formerly known as the 'Accounts form' had been replaced by a new form called the 'Computer form', in fact no additional work was being undertaken by the branch. He did find, however, that the branch had to complete no fewer than six forms, two of them in triplicate and one in quadruplicate. In one case the same piece of data was entered on every form – a total, including the carbon copies, of thirteen times. In many other cases the same entries were copied on to four or more forms.

At the next opportunity the director challenged John Fane on this work and was told that he would look into it.

## PROBLEMS

1. What in your opinion was wrong with the method used in John Fane's presentation of the new system to the Board?

2. Have you any criticisms of the contents of the proposal?

3. Do you agree with the reason given by John Fane for keeping the project a secret? Why do you think the three clerks left the company at Christmas?

4. If you had been in charge of the project, what would you have done?

# 2 Payroll

*A case study by F. W. Purchall*

## INTRODUCTION

This application has become a 'stock' feature of almost every data-processing installation – so much so that there is now available a wide choice of 'packages' which will in most cases obviate to a large extent the task of systems design and programming. The following case study is not intended to illustrate a typical payroll procedure, but to introduce the reader to the need for several sort runs when operating transaction and master files on magnetic tape. The case study has been deliberately kept simple, with none of the complications which would normally be associated with an industrial payroll.

The reader will be expected to have a good knowledge of the operation of a magnetic-tape-based system and some of the requirements for a payroll procedure, in particular the need for close control, for accuracy and for speed of operation. For example, the master file must be accurate and up to date before the calculation of wages. Similarly, provision must be made for the immediate correction of any errors on the main run. It would not be acceptable for an employee to have to wait a week for his wages owing to an error being corrected for input next week.

## CASE STUDY

Bodgers Ltd, a medium-sized firm of builders and decorators, engaged mainly in maintenance work, pay all their employees on a straight time-work basis. Each employee completes a weekly time sheet, showing the time spent on a particular job, with details of overtime hours. This time sheet is signed by the site foreman or clerk of works, and it is then sent to the main office for the calculation of wages. After the preparation of the payroll, the cash is made up into envelopes together with a pay-slip giving the details of make-up of net pay, and these are then taken to the various sites and distributed by the site foreman or clerk of works to the men. Each man, apart from labourers, is a tradesman, working for an agreed hourly rate of pay, and he will never undertake work outside of his trade; for example, a carpenter will under no circumstances lay bricks or paint the woodwork he has just finished. Similarly, the labourers are not allowed to do any 'trade' work; their job is to lift, carry, shovel, etc. Overtime rates are always time and a half, except on Sundays and Bank Holidays, when double time is paid. There are a maximum of fifty 'trade' categories. Each man is allocated an employee number which remains the same throughout his employment, even if he is promoted to a foreman's job; furthermore this number is never reissued, even when the man leaves the employment of the company.

Each maintenance job accepted by the company is also allocated a unique number which is not reused. Clerks of works and site foremen are given instructions by head office on Friday afternoons on the detailing of men to site jobs for the following week. In practice emergencies are always arising, and although a man may have been allocated to a particular job on the Monday, he could well be called to another job on Wednesday, but for the purpose of this case study we shall assume that a man allocated to a site job on the Monday will always remain there for the rest of the week.

The number of employees averages 10,000, but on average some 10 per cent of them will be given a new site job to work on each week.

To enable job costing to be readily prepared, the payroll master file is to be maintained in job-number sequence, and within each job-number block of records the employee records are held in employee-number sequence. This is also helpful in preparing the coinage analysis, which is done by job as well as in total to provide a check on 'bagging up' the wages each week.

The company has a computer installation, at present used for stock control, with the following configuration:

A central processor with 32 K characters of core store.
Console typewriter.
Card reader operating at 900 cards per minute.
Line printer operating at 1,250 lines per minute with 160 print positions.
Card punch operating at 250 cards per minute.
All peripherals fully buffered.
A magnetic tape cluster of six tape decks operating at 20 Kc.

Management have decided to transfer the payroll procedure to the computer, mainly to speed up payroll preparation, which at the moment is taking far too long and is furthermore subject to a high peak of work on one day a week. They also intend to use the computer for the production of work-in-progress and job costing.

The main weekly outputs required are therefore:

Printed payroll.
Printed payslips each of four lines.
Accumulated totals of work-in-progress per job by trade and in total.
Coinage analysis by job and by total.
File containing each employee's pay record together with the total labour cost to date for each job.

The average number of site jobs being undertaken at any one time is 200, but this figure is subject to considerable fluctuations. For example, on occasion some very large jobs are accepted, and these will occupy a large proportion of the labour force.

## PROBLEMS

1. Prepare computer flowcharts (run diagrams) showing the weekly runs required to completion of the payroll, payslips and coinage analysis.

2. Prepare outline record designs for punched-card input and for the master file.

3. Prepare provisional designs for payslip and payroll.

# 3 Random Interrogation of a Large File

*A case study on information retrieval by F. W. Purchall*

# INTRODUCTION

All businesses are concerned with the problem of obtaining information quickly. In some cases the time scale is instantaneous; for example, the catalyst plant of an oil refinery. In other cases immediacy, while not essential, is nevertheless desirable; for example, a credit customer of a departmental store will be prepared to wait, say, five minutes for the information regarding her account, but not for an hour.

One of the problems associated with the processing of data on a computer is the need to obtain information from a large file to satisfy random inquiries. There are broadly four approaches to this problem:

1. Processing in real-time.
2. Batch processing, using an interrogating typewriter to interrupt the main program or programs to deal with inquiries.
3. Batch processing, interspersed with batched inquiries.
4. Batch processing coupled with a complete historical print-out of the file.

The choice of method must depend on the amount of time which can be reasonably allowed between the inquiry and the information, conditioned by the cost involved.

In working the following case study it will be assumed that the reader has a reasonable knowledge of computer systems, including hardware and software capabilities. It will also be necessary for the reader to have a clear understanding of the method of accounting used by hire-purchase companies.

The case study poses a similar problem to the case study on Cash Collection (pp. 35–43 below). The main differences are:

(a) The Cash Collection case assumes the availability of a large computing system, whereas this case relies on a minimum configuration and rules out the use of expensive peripherals such as optical character readers and direct storage devices.

(b) Whilst both cases are concerned with cash collection, the real problem associated with this case is one of interrogation.

## CASE STUDY

This case study is based on a well-known finance company specialising in the provision of finance for hire-purchase, mainly for automobiles, but increasingly in recent years covering most of the larger consumer products. A recent development has been the provision of hire-purchase finance in the industrial field, including agriculture. The company has for some years processed all data on conventional punched-card equipment, and is now considering the installation of a digital computer.

It will be appreciated that the main purpose of hire-purchase accounting is to maintain strict credit control. The routine reporting arising from the state of each account is not a statement sent out at regular intervals as in a sales accounting procedure, but a succession of arrears notices, each being sent when an account is overdue by a certain number of days.

Terminology is also somewhat different in hire-purchase accounting; for example, 'balance' is the amount still to be paid if the contract runs its course, and must be distinguished from 'arrears' which is the amount actually owing at any particular time.

When a due-day comes around for an account, the value of the instalment due is taken off the 'balance' and put to 'arrears'. As and when cash is received from the client, this is deducted from the 'arrears', and not from the 'balance'. Thus a prompt payer will have his 'arrears' raised and cancelled in the same pass of data. Should a client pay cash to the company before the due date he will create 'negative arrears' in his

19

account, which will be cancelled on the next due day, when the next instalment is taken from the 'balance' and put to 'arrears'.

A study of the present system disclosed the following facts, all of which will be maintained for the foreseeable future:

1. From the total cost of the product, the client is required to pay in cash a deposit. To the net amount is added a percentage to cover loan interest and administrative charges. This figure is the balance.
2. Instalments are charged each calendar month, the 'balance' being divided by 12, 24 or 36, dependent upon the period of the hire-purchase, to arrive at the amount of the instalment. Very few instalment periods run for more than one year, and for simplicity you are asked to ignore periods in excess of one year.
3. Each account is allocated a digital number which is unique to that account and is never reused. The maximum number of accounts in current operation is 200,000.
4. The due date of each account is the day of the month on which the first instalment falls due; for example, for a client opening an account on 3 January, the first instalment will be due on 3 February, and subsequent instalments on 3 March, 3 April, etc., except that instalments cannot fall due on a Saturday or a Sunday.
5. In order that the load of accounting and clerical work can be spread, an account is examined for arrears on the fourteenth, the twenty-eighth and the thirty-second day after its due date.
6. Business is done through five branches within a radius of thirty miles of head office, as well as through head office direct.

The data-processing requirements are:

1. The daily updating of the accounts file from returns of cash received by the branches.
2. The preparation daily of a listing of cash received (Cash Received book) for head office.
3. A daily print-out of accounts in arrear and arrears paid for head office.

4. For the branches a list of accounts in arrear and arrears paid for daily dispatch to branches.
5. A means whereby clerks can refer to the file at short notice to find the 'settlement figure' for any account. Clients get tired of paying the instalments or perhaps have a 'windfall' and will call at their branch, or at head office, personally or by telephone, to 'settle' their account. The 'settlement' figure is arrived at by taking the 'balance', the value of the instalments still outstanding, and removing from it the 'charges' element (interest, administration costs) which would normally be included in these instalments. It is obvious therefore that the file must be kept strictly up to date.

CONSTRAINTS IMPOSED BY THE COMPANY

The hire-purchase accounting project will be the main job for the computer. The only other job being considered is payroll, and as this is a simple salaried procedure, it is expected to take a minimal amount of machine time. Because of this the company is looking for as economical a configuration of machine as is practicable, which rules out the use of direct-access storage devices and data-transmission networks.

## PROBLEMS

1. What configuration of machine do you recommend?

2. What method will you use to provide for quick and easy reference to the file?

# 4 Production Scheduling

*A case study by F. W. Purchall*

## INTRODUCTION

This subject is one which forms part of a production planning and control system. Such a system in a manufacturing business, e.g. engineering, becomes extremely complex, involving as it does the breakdown from sales order requirements to the basic factors of men, machines, parts and raw materials, followed by the scheduling of the work-load on to the plant and the consequential feedback control loop to check on results and modify future plans. An essential factor in all such systems is *time* because the system is a dynamic one, subject to constant change. It follows therefore that the smaller the time-lag which elapses between the preparation of the plan and its communication to the factory floor, the greater will be the likelihood of the plan being achieved. The following case study does not attempt to cover such a complex system, but it is hoped that the importance of speed of processing will become obvious to the reader.

The reader will be expected to have a reasonable understanding of file processing on magnetic tapes, and is advised to do some reading on alternative methods of data capture.


## CASE STUDY

Burke Bakeries Ltd, well known for their brand of B.B. bread, are wholesale bakers. Their products are distributed in two ways:

(a) parcel deliveries to some 300 retailers;
(b) by a fleet of 150 of their own vans, also to retailers, within an area of twenty-five miles of the bakery.

The maximum number of products is 170, of which 70 are bread and 100 are cakes and pastries, known in the trade as flour confectionery. All flour confectionery, together with a certain amount of bread, is baked on the day shift, which works from 8 a.m. to 5 p.m. The amount of bread baked is dependent entirely on the spare capacity available after scheduling the flour confectionery. During the night shift only bread is baked.

The products are obviously very perishable; the shelf life of flour confectionery can be three to four days, dependent on the weather and other conditions, but bread must be fresh and therefore be sold on the same day. The amount of bread to be baked on the night shift must therefore be determined with care and accuracy.

The following is a description of the existing manual system. A file is in existence for parcel orders, showing the standing order from each retailer for each day of the week from Monday to Saturday, together with a production schedule of each day's orders. If a retailer wishes to change his order for any day, he must notify the office by 4 p.m. at least two working days before the day in question. The production schedule is amended to take account of these amendments and subsequently invoices are prepared. There are an average of twelve items per invoice, and on average 5 per cent of customers amend their orders each day, so that amendments received by 4 p.m. on Monday will be used to plan the production on the day shift on Tuesday, and will be dispatched to retailers Wednesday morning. The company will not accept any returns from these customers, and any complaints regarding the quality of goods dispatched result in the replacement of the goods on the next possible delivery.

Sales via the company's van are different. The van-men deliver the goods, collect the cash, and take orders for future delivery. The van-men are therefore more than a delivery service, they are also salesmen. In fact they are expected to sell all the goods taken by them each morning, and are actively discouraged from bringing back unsold items. They are expected to place their orders daily with care and accuracy as follows:

(*a*) Bread products for delivery the following day.
(*b*) Flour confectionery for delivery two days ahead.

Owing to the different distances involved on each round, the first van-men arrive at the office to place their orders and pay in their cash at around noon, the last van-man does not check in until 4 p.m. The average number of items ordered each day by the van-men is 70, with a maximum for any one item of 300. Effectively, therefore, the company sells goods to the van-men, the van-men receiving a commission on sales in addition to their wages. If goods are not sold, the van-man loses the value of the goods as the company will not normally accept returns (except in the case of goods damaged in transit or outdated goods). As the van-men return to the office they complete two pre-printed order forms, one for bread and the other for flour confectionery. These order forms are built up on a peg-board, and cross-totalled to arrive at the production schedule. The work-load, however, is subject to a peak as approximately two-thirds of the van-men arrive between 3.30 p.m. and 4 p.m. and the production schedule must be completed before 5 p.m., when the office closes.

The company have a computer and require a system to be devised which will provide for the preparation of invoices and delivery notes for parcels deliveries; the preparation of the van-men's order advice which will show the description of each commodity loaded, the quantity, price and value; one order advice for bread and another for flour confectionery; a daily statement of account for the van-men, showing sales returns, cash paid in, balance outstanding and accumulated sales for the month for the calculation of commission; an analysis of orders which must show the quantity of bread to be baked on the night shift, after taking into account the amount of bread baked during the day shift, and the amount of flour confectionery to be baked during the following day shift; during these analyses the quantities of each commodity to be sent to each of five loading bays to be determined; stock control and raw material requirements for production on each shift to be calculated and the details sent to the storekeeper so that he can load hoppers before the shift starts.

The machine at present installed has:

a 16 K word core store, each word=24 bits=4 chars;
punched paper tape input operating at 1,000 characters per second;
six magnetic-tape decks operating at 20·8 Kch/sec;
line printer operating at 600 lines/minute;
simultaneity on all peripherals.

The company is prepared to consider an alternative form of input to the computer should it prove desirable, but is not otherwise prepared to change the configuration of the machine.

## PROBLEMS

1. Design in outline the required outputs.

2. Design the form and method of input.

3. Draw up computer flowcharts showing the computer runs and peripherals used.

4. Time the run concerned with the analysis of van-men's orders for production scheduling.

# 5 Integrated Data Processing

*A case study by F. W. Purchall*

## INTRODUCTION

It is a truism to state that every business transaction, however small, has repercussions throughout the data-processing system. It has long been the ambition of computer technologists to provide a fully integrated system on a computer, sometimes referred to as the 'one-shot approach', whereby each transaction will update every file affected by it, resulting in an immediate amendment of the final accounts. The imagination is fired by the prospect of the Managing Director being able to call up at any moment the up-to-date position of his company, for example the Profit and Loss account, on a video display unit in his office. This prospect is not so far away as many people think; already one large manufacturer of computers is rapidly approaching this objective. At the present moment managers can interrogate files relating to their responsibilities by remote terminals or video display units.

For obvious reasons the following case study is not so ambitious, but it does presuppose the integration of the revenue accounting of a company with a simple stock control routine, together with the preparation of some basic management information in the form of sales statistics.

The reader of the case study will be expected to have an understanding of batch processing, the design of punched cards and the layout of records on magnetic tape.

## CASE STUDY

Wallcoverings Ltd, manufacturers of wallpaper and vinyl-coated wall coverings, are already the proud possessors of a computer, used at present for payroll and labour costing.

30

The machine has the following configuration: card reader reading 80-column cards at 600 cards per minute; line printer operating at 1,200 lines per minute for normal spacing at six lines to the inch, but for spacing of eight lines or more there is a fast skip at the rate of 4,800 lines a minute, 120 print positions; and a cluster of four magnetic-tape decks operating at 90 K characters but connected by only two channels to the central processor. The tape decks have a 7 m.s. start/stop time. Attached to the processor on a high-speed channel is an exchangeable disc drive with the following facilities: character transfer rate 156 Kc, latency time 9 m.s., 10 tracks to a cylinder, 200 tracks per disc, track capacity 3,600 characters. The arm movement, which can normally take place outside of processor time, is minimum 12 m.s., maximum 150 m.s. The capacity of the store is 128 Kc and there is a console typewriter which operates at 10 characters/second. All slow-speed peripherals are fully buffered.

The company now wish to transfer their sales accounting and invoice preparation to the computer and, as a result of a feasibility study, management have agreed that it would be desirable to link this application with the control of the stock. This will, it is hoped, ensure that invoices will be prepared only when stock is available. Following upon the feasibility study, a detailed analysis of the present system was made, when it became apparent that there were further advantages to be obtained from the system in the form of sales statistics. Management have therefore agreed on the following outputs:

*Daily*
(a) The production of invoices after checking for stock availability. Orders frustrated by stock-outs to be carried forward for input the next day.
(b) The updating of the customer's account.
(c) The production of statistics of the value of sales for each area.

*Monthly*
(a) The production of statements for dispatch to customers.
(b) The production of statistics of the value of sales by area for each commodity.

(*c*) The production of statistics of the value of sales by commodity for each area.

(*d*) The production of statistics of the value of sales for each customer analysed by commodity.

(*e*) The production of the value of sales per representative for commission purposes.

The analysis of the present system disclosed that the average number of invoices produced each day was 3,000, but the number could fall as low as 1,000 during the winter months, and rise as high as 5,000 in the spring and early summer. The average number of commodity items per invoice was two, and in fact some 50 per cent of invoices carried only one commodity item. All commodity items are subject to purchase tax of 10 per cent. Trade discount is allowed on the price of the commodity in five ranges according to the trade group of the customer. The ranges are 20 per cent, 15 per cent, 10 per cent, 5 per cent and 2½ per cent. Cash discount is not allowed. There are 5,000 patterns in the catalogue, each pattern identified by a six-digit numerical code. Alpha descriptions are not used, customers ordering by pattern number. The price range varies from 30p to £12. Wall coverings are sold by the piece (roll) and there is a wide range of order quantities with a maximum of 99.

Goods are dispatched by road, rail, sea, air or by post. Method of dispatch is determined by the size of the consignment, unless a special request is made by the customer, e.g. urgent orders when requested will be sent by air, passenger train or by express post. If a customer does not make a special request, then the method is determined in the office, and a charge is made as follows: Retailers for orders over £5, no charge; for orders of £5 or less the charge is 15p. Wholesalers for orders over £10, no charge; for orders of £10 or less, the actual charge. In the case of special dispatches the actual charge is always made. A charge for carriage appears on approximately 40 per cent of all invoices.

On approximately 30 per cent of all invoices, the customer requires the name and address of a consignee. This is required by the customer for reference purposes only, and can therefore be kept to a maximum of 28 characters on the invoice. A separate label is prepared manually for the dispatch of the goods.

In addition to the pattern number, which is unique to the pattern, there are 40 different commodity codes, forming commodity groups; for example, ceiling papers, wallpaper printed, wallpaper embossed, wallpaper flocked, vinyl papers, etc.

There are 400 sales areas in the country, each area being the responsibility of a sales representative. These areas have been arranged so that each representative has approximately the same number of customers, with a larger number allocated to representatives in large towns, and a correspondingly smaller number for representatives in rural areas. The average number of accounts which move each month is 30,000 out of a total customer list of approximately 60,000. The average cash-received transactions per month are 30,000.

Management have decided that in addition to the normal requirements of an invoice the following information must appear:

(a) Invoice number (six digits).
(b) Date of the invoice.
(c) Trade terms (trade discount allowed).
(d) Customer account number (eight digits).
(e) Customer order number or date of order (six digits).
(f) Our own order number (six digits).
(g) Method of dispatch.

## PROBLEMS

1. Prepare a provisional forms design for the invoice and the monthly statement.

2. Prepare provisional card designs and file layouts.

3. Prepare computer flowcharts (run diagrams) for daily and monthly runs, bearing in mind the restrictions imposed by the configuration of machine available.

4. Prepare an approximate timing for the daily and monthly runs, ignoring for this purpose any timings for sorts.

33

# 6 Cash Collection: Castle Rock Insurance Group

*A case study by Raymond S. Walker*

## INTRODUCTION

This case study covers the design of a cash-collection system. It is based on a solution adopted by a large insurance group, but would be applicable to any organisation receiving large numbers of payments by post. Public utilities and local authorities are examples of organisations likely to have similar problems.

The study demonstrates the need to consider whether it is possible to modify the task to be performed to facilitate a more economical solution. It also illustrates some aspects of costing the implementation and operation of a system.

The study assumes familiarity with various forms of computer input and the relative costs.

## CASE STUDY

The Castle Rock Insurance Group has been formed by a series of mergers and take-overs. It now consists of nine companies, each issuing policies in their separate names.

The Group transacts business in the United Kingdom through sixty branch offices employing 6,000 staff. It earns a yearly premium income of about £50 million from 3 million policies with premiums ranging from £2 to £75,000.

The majority of policies are renewable annually, a high proportion on one of the four English quarter days, 25 March, 24 June, 29 September and 25 December.

The premiums on about 1·5 million policies are paid by post to the branch offices of the company, a small number in cash over the branch office counters, and the remainder are collected by agents who account quarterly to their local branch.

Although policies are issued in the names of the separate companies, their separate identities have otherwise been lost within the organisation. They all use the same staff and offices, and common systems are in use.

A computer has been used for a number of years for the production of statistics, and to print notices for policies due for renewal. These notices have been sent in bulk to agents and branches for dispatch to the insured.

The computer records are held on magnetic tape and updated weekly from advices completed by the branches.

Many insured review their policies at renewal so that a high proportion of premiums are changed. This has deterred the Group from mechanising its premium collection and accounting so that accounting, and the dispatch of reminders for unpaid premiums, remain a manual process performed by branch staff.

Rising salaries, the rapidly increasing size of the Group and the importance of collecting premiums as quickly as possible, to achieve the maximum possible investment income, make it desirable to review existing procedures, and a small group of systems analysts has been set up with the following brief:

1. Examine the existing procedures for receiving and accounting for renewal premiums.
2. Recommend any changes in existing manual procedures.
3. Consider the advantages, and disadvantages, of centralising the collection of cash, and if no serious disadvantages are apparent, design a system in outline and provide an estimate of costs for comparison with existing methods.

Very early in their investigation the team concluded that handling cash from the public was a completely different problem from receiving cash from the agents. They decided to concentrate initially on the former, but they first established that the information necessary for accounting purposes was the same for premiums collected direct, and from agents, namely:

| Branch | 3 numeric characters |
| Agency | 4 numeric and 1 alpha character |
| Group company | 1 numeric character |
| Policy number | 10 alpha numeric characters |

Reference date of debit  5 numeric characters DDDYY,
                         where DDD = day of year
Amount of debit          7 numeric characters ££££££.pp

The examination of existing procedures for payments collected direct from the insured elicited the following information:

1. Renewals are printed monthly with a reminder as a carbon copy. Both notice and reminder have a counterfoil which the insured is asked to return with the remittance.
2. A list is printed at the same time, showing:
   (a) branch
   (b) agency
   (c) Group company
   (d) policy number
   (e) reference date of debit
   (f) name of insured
   (g) amount of premium
   (h) amount of commission
   (i) net amount due
   (j) date due
   (k) sequence reference.
   The list is printed in sequence reference order and the same reference appears on the renewal notices and counterfoils.
3. As premiums are paid, the list is date-stamped, and the amount is entered by hand in a cash book. The cash book entry shows items (a) to (d) above, together with the net amount paid and the date. The premiums on several policies are often paid with a single cheque.
4. Cheques, postal orders and cash are banked daily and the cash book regularly balanced with the bank statement. The balance on the account is transferred weekly to the head office account, from which it is invested.
5. About fourteen days after the end of the month, reminders are sent for any items which are not date-stamped. The reminders for date-stamped items are destroyed.

   The team noted that, although the reminder was sent fourteen days after the renewal date of policies renewable at the end of the month, policies renewable at the beginning of the month were then six weeks overdue. It was also noted that on some days premiums for three months were being paid, the previous month paid late, the current month and the following month paid early.

6. Receipts are not issued unless specially requested, when the counterfoil is rubber-stamped, signed and returned to the insured. Motor certificates are issued for most motor policies and prompt dispatch is important.

7. Where premiums remain unpaid fourteen days after sending the reminder, the list is initialled by a responsible official and a letter sent to the insured advising him that his policy has lapsed.

While carrying out their analysis of existing procedures, the team learnt that a number of uncrossed postal orders had been stolen by a clerk at one of the branches.

He had concealed his theft by marking up the cases as paid on the following day, and using payments received that following day to achieve a balance with the cash book.

The defalcation was discovered when the clerk was taken ill suddenly, and by this time he was using a high proportion of payments on any one day to clear items which should have been marked as paid the previous day.

The team also discovered that there were no costings available for cash collection. There appeared to be about two people employed on this work at most branches, but around quarter days the number was increased.

The peaks were dealt with at branches by transferring staff from other work, and allowing work to fall into arrear, but this solution would not be acceptable for central operations where only very limited variations in the number of staff could be tolerated.

Inquiries established that policies were renewable on quarter days for historical reasons, and that little objection to changing the dates could be expected from most insured, provided they were not inconvenienced or asked to pay more.

Quantities of stationery used for renewals sent direct to insured during the last twelve months were:

| | |
|---|---|
| January | 50,000 |
| February | 50,000 |
| March | 300,000 |
| April | 70,000 |
| May | 60,000 |
| June | 255,000 |
| July | 60,000 |
| August | 55,000 |
| September | 230,000 |
| October | 70,000 |
| November | 42,000 |
| December | 266,000 |
| | 1,508,000 |

It was clear that the large volume of renewals due on the four quarter days could be embarrassing, and it was decided to investigate the pattern of payments at a number of branch offices. The distribution seemed to depend on a number of factors; for example, in some areas people tended to pay their premiums at weekends.

From figures that were obtained it was concluded that, although the average number of remittances to be processed would be 6,000 per day, that is 1·5 million per annum spread over 250 working days, the number in practice would range between 2,000 and 14,000 per day.

The March renewals were about to be printed and the program was modified to analyse the distribution of premiums with the following results:

| | No. of policies | Total premium |
|---|---|---|
| Premiums of £2 (the minimum charged) | 95,000 | £190,000 |
| Premiums over £2 up to £3 | 55,000 | 130,000 |
| Premiums over £3 up to £4 | 40,000 | 140,000 |
| Premiums over £4 up to £5 | 38,000 | 165,000 |
| Premiums over £5 up to £10 | 35,000 | 300,000 |
| Premiums over £10 up to £50 | 15,000 | 600,000 |
| Premiums over £50 | 20,000 | 1,600,000 |
| | 298,000 | £3,125,000 |

It seemed reasonable to assume that the other quarter months would follow the same pattern.

The systems analysts then had preliminary talks with a representative of their bank who assured them that arrangements could be made to process through one branch the volumes they envisaged, although the wide variation in numbers would be an embarrassment to the bank also.

They also talked to National Giro, and were particularly interested in an offer by Giro to provide them with particulars of items credited through the National Giro system on magnetic tape. If a suitable counterfoil was sent with the notice with a code line printed on it by the Group's computer for use by the Giro optical reader, the charge was nominal.

It seemed that 6 per cent to 10 per cent of items might be paid this way.

A suggestion that Giro should collect all premiums, whether paid by Giro or cheque, was not acceptable to the Castle Rock Insurance Group for political reasons.

Finally, the systems analysts ascertained that a partition of 90 K characters could be made available on the computer for up to six hours per day. The computer would be performing other programs simultaneously and the book cost for the partition would be £30 per hour. Tape and disc drives would be available together with a 1,100-line-per-minute printer, and a card reader/punch.

The team could ascertain no objection, in principle, to centralising the collection of cash, and proceeded to design a suitable system in outline in order to arrive at comparative costs. They felt that perhaps the most important feature of the system was that of data preparation, and they considered the following methods of data input:

(a) Paper tape, punched cards, magnetic tape or direct input keyed by an operator. The variation of volume of input presented problems.

(b) A card pre-punched by the computer and sent with the renewal notice. They anticipated difficulties in associating the correct punched card and notice. They also thought that a high proportion of cards might be mutilated.

(c) A card pre-punched by the computer which would also be printed with the notice particulars. There was some doubt as to how this could be produced and whether it would be acceptable to the public. There was also the likelihood of mutilation.

(d) A counterfoil attached to the notice pre-encoded by the computer for a mark sense reader. There were difficulties in coding the required information on a counterfoil of acceptable size.

(e) A counterfoil attached to the notice pre-encoded by the computer for an optical reader. Some of the optical readers could also read constrained handwritten figures. One machine they considered, which rented at £1,500 per month, was capable of reading 6,000 documents per hour. The cost and need to provide protection against misread characters were the only disadvantages.

## PROBLEMS

1. Consider how the manual system could be improved and suggest any alternatives.

2 (i) Design in outline and describe a computer-based system to perform the work required as listed below.

(ii) Provide rough drafts of any documents required.

(iii) Estimate the costs of implementing and operating the system you propose, and compare the proposal with the existing situation.

The system should cover the following aspects:

(a) Identification, or separation of postal remittances from other post, as far as possible before the envelopes are opened.

(b) Opening envelopes and removal of contents.

(c) Manual procedures for handling remittances.

(d) Computer system providing:
   (1) input to accounting suite;
   (2) reconciliation of input to accounting suite with cheques, postal orders and Giro transfers.

(e) Banking remittances, and reconciliation of the bank balance with the input to the accounting suite.

The production of reminders for unpaid premiums was to be carried out by the accounting suite and need not be included in the proposal.

Should you discover you lack any information, state how you would obtain it, and make reasonable assumptions.

It you decide to use an optical reader or other device which has to be used on line to a computer, you may assume that the computer which is available is suitable.

# Guidelines

## HUMAN FACTORS

All human beings are resistant to change, and this applies equally to the Board of Directors and to the clerk. A proposal submitted to a Board with 'a loaded pistol pointed at their heads' will result in a snap decision, but will build up resentment and suspicion. The proposal should have been submitted several months earlier and every opportunity given for full discussion. The contents of the proposal were far too vague – no one at the meeting had a real understanding of what was being proposed, and the costings presented were incomplete; for example, no real alternative was given to the proposed computer system.

No new system will work efficiently without the full co-operation of the staff. It follows therefore that every effort must be made by the systems analyst to overcome their natural resistance to change. This can be done by keeping them in the picture from the outset and involving them by consulting them and getting them to participate by making suggestions. Ignorance will breed fear and suspicion, rumour will become rife, and it is possible that the best members of staff will leave because it is easier for them to get other work. It is important to provide one of the basic motivators – security. If redundancy is inevitable, then staff should be told and a measure of security given in the form of generous severance pay.

The project was ill-planned from the start, and the short answer to problem 4 is 'Plan'. If the project had been carefully planned and a proper fact-finding analysis had taken place, then undoubtedly the computer system could have started much further back in the accounting system, thus relieving the branches of much detailed work.

Suggested reading: E. Mumford and T. B. Ward, *Computers: Planning for People* (Batsford, 1968).

## PAYROLL

Although the questions raised in this case study relate to the data-processing aspect only, it is important to remember that the systems analyst is responsible for the total system design, including that part of the system which functions outside of the computer department. Equally he is responsible for establishing effective controls, and he must therefore plan for essential feedback to ensure that the system operates satisfactorily and does not permit the introduction of errors or the practice of fraud on the business. This control function is important in all data-processing applications, but nowhere is it more important than in a payroll application.

Before we consider the possible solutions to the questions, it may be useful to spend a little time on considering how control can be established outside of the computer department. The biggest risks are the introduction of fictitious employees on to the payroll and the payment to bona fide employees for hours not worked. In order that these risks can be safeguarded but not necessarily entirely eliminated, the usual plan is to divide up the duties involved in the preparation of the payroll. For example, notification of changes to the master file for new employees, leavers, revisions of pay rates, changes in deductions and exemptions, promotions, etc., should be the responsibility of the personnel department. Transfers to new sites should be the responsibility of a planning manager, who should notify site foremen, as well as the data-processing department. The making up of wages and the handling of the cash should be the duty of the cashier. The payment of wages is already the job of the site foreman, so that there would have to be collusion among many staff to perpetrate a fraud.

As far as the data-processing system is concerned, two important factors must be considered by the systems analyst: (*a*) the need for great accuracy as nothing is more inclined to disrupt industrial relations than receiving incorrect pay, and

(b) the time element – frustrated sales orders can be held over and re-input on the next run, but wages must be paid when due.

It is suggested that the reader starts with problem 3. Until a provisional design for the payslip is drawn up, it will be difficult to consider the design of input. Similarly the design of the payroll and job-costing analysis will determine the content of file records. Compare your draft with Appendix 2.3, but do not change your draft unless it is on the face of it so different as to appear to be incorrect. It is better for the reader to design his own system from start to finish and then compare it with the suggested solution than repeatedly to change his own thoughts to keep in step with mine.

Now proceed to problem 2 and design the punched cards required for input, together with the records to be held on the file. Two card types are required. One will amend the main file to bring it up to date before the actual payroll run for all changes, i.e. new employees, leavers, changes in existing employees' records – e.g. revised tax code number – and for the cases where men are transferred to a new site. Whilst it would seem logical to design a different card for each of the above conditions, in the actual company one card type only was used, but in the majority of amendments only three fields were punched – employee number, current job number and new job number. When designing this card you can design the employee record to be held on the payroll master file, which apart from accumulative fields must contain most if not all of the data in this card.

The other input card should be comparatively easy to design, consisting as it does mainly of details of time worked. This record will be quite short, so consider using a 'spread' card. In the actual case each card contained three employee time-sheet records, which reduced the number of cards on the payroll run from 10,000 to approximately 3,333, nearly four minutes for card reader time.

As the master file is organised sequentially by job number, it would seem reasonable to keep the job-costing analysis as a 'trailer' record at the end of the employee records for each job number. The analysis could then be updated during the payroll run and printed out at the conclusion of each job payroll (see Appendices 2.2 and 2.3).

The computer runs are shown in Appendix 2.4 and consist of preliminary runs 01 to 05 followed by the main runs 06 to 08. The preliminary runs are concerned with amendments to the master file. The main features are:

(a) The requirement of run 01, whereby we do not proceed to run 02 until all amendments have been correctly written to the file.

(b) That in run 03 the records of employees who have been moved to a new site must be deleted from the master file before writing to the new master, and written instead to a transfer or changes file. This file must then be sorted to the new job-number sequence so that the records can be reinserted into the master file in run 05 in their correct sequence. Note the print-out in run 03, a copy of which will be sent to the personnel department as confirmation of action taken, and the print-out in run 05 for confirmation with the planning manager. These print-outs, together with the validity checks and control total checks, are part of the systems control.

The main runs are a straightforward data vet, sort, update sequence. Again it is important that all time-sheet data should be corrected and written to the file before proceeding to the sort run (run 06). Run 08 is a match of time-sheet data with the master file, the calculation of pay and printing of the payslip, the updating of the master, including the labour job-cost analysis records, and the writing of this file to the new master. Provision must be made for the possibility of a time sheet being prepared for a new employee whose details have not come through from the personnel department. His record will not therefore appear on the master file. This resulting mismatch has been catered for by punching out the details of the employee's time-sheet data into a punched card. In practice the number of cards falling into this category each week was of the order of two or three, and these were dealt with manually after confirmation with the personnel department. If the number became excessive, it would become necessary either to improve the system of notification by the personnel department, or to provide for a rerun of runs 01 to 08. It is obvious which would be the better step to take.

Before run 09 the master-file tape will have to be rewound; the run consists of a straightforward tape to printer, printing the payroll from the employee records and the labour job-cost analysis at the end of each job number (see Appendix 2.3). This could be a 'spooling' run on many machines.

Owing to the small-sized core store, the suite of programs is held on magnetic tape, each segment of program being called in as required.

APPENDIX 2.1

PUNCHED CARD INPUT

ADDITIONS, DELETIONS AND AMENDMENTS

| Card Type | Emp. No. | Name | Previous Job No. | New Job No. | Trade | Tax code | Std. hrly. rate | N.I. rate | Grad. Pen. rate p/w | Sav-ings p/w | Other deds. p/w | Holi-day credit p/w | Addition Deletion Amendment |
|---|---|---|---|---|---|---|---|---|---|---|---|---|---|
| No. of cols. 1 | 6 | 20 | 6 | 6 | 2 | 3 | 3 | 3 | 3 | 3 | 3 | 3 | 1 |

63 columns. For amendments, fields punched are Emp. No. and fields to be amended.

TIME-SHEET CARD

| Card Type | Emp. No. | Current Job No. | Normal hours | Normal o/time hours | Special o/time hours |
|---|---|---|---|---|---|
| 1 | 6 | 6 | 4 | 4 | 4 |

No. of cols.

24 columns per record
3 records per card.

## APPENDIX 2.2
### FILE RECORDS: MAGNETIC TAPE PAYROLL MASTER FILE
#### EMPLOYEE RECORD

| | Job No. | Emp. No. | Job No. | Name | Standard hourly rate | Tax code | Total gross pay to date | Total tax to date | N.I. contribution | Grad. Pension to date |
|---|---|---|---|---|---|---|---|---|---|---|
| No. of Chars. | 6 | 6 | 6 | 20 | 3 | 3 | 6 | 6 | 3 | 3 |

| | | | | | | | | PAYROLL THIS WEEK | | | |
|---|---|---|---|---|---|---|---|---|---|---|---|
| | Savings p/w | Holiday credit p/w | Savings to date | Holiday credits to date | Trade code | Total hours | Gross pay | Tax paid/refund | G.P.S. | Deds. | Holiday credit | Net pay |
| No. of Chars. | 3 | 3 | 4 | 5 | 2 | 4 | 4 | 3 | 3 | 3 | 3 | 4 |

#### JOB COST RECORD
(one record for each job)

| | Job No. | Trade 01 | Value | Trade 02 | Value | --- | Trade 50 | Value |
|---|---|---|---|---|---|---|---|---|
| No. of Chars. | 6 | 2 | 6 | 2 | 6 | | 2 | 6 |

# APPENDIX 2.3

## PAYSLIP

| BODGERs LTD | | | | | | | PAY ADVICE | |
|---|---|---|---|---|---|---|---|---|
| Name | Emp. No. | Week No. | Tax code | Hourly rate | Normal hours | Normal O/T hours | Special O/T hours | Holiday credit |
| Pay normal hours | Pay O/T hours (N) | Pay O/T hours (S) | | Holiday pay | | | | Gross pay |
| Grad. Pension | Tax this week | Savings this week | | Nat. Ins. | | | | Total deductions |
| Holiday credit to date | Gross pay to date | | | Tax to date | | | | Net pay |

## PAYROLL

Job No. _____

| Emp. No. | Trade | Hrs. | Gross | Tax | N.I. | G.P.S. | Deds. | Total Deds. | Holiday credit | Net | Week No. |
|---|---|---|---|---|---|---|---|---|---|---|---|
| —— | —— | —— | —— | —— | —— | —— | —— | —— | —— | —— | |

*Job Coinage Analysis*

| | | £5 | £1 | 50p | 10p | 5p | Copper | | | | |
|---|---|---|---|---|---|---|---|---|---|---|---|

*Job Cost to Date*

Job No.

| Trade | 01 | | | | | | | | | | Week No. |
|---|---|---|---|---|---|---|---|---|---|---|---|
| Cost | 02 | 03 | 04 | —— | —— | | | | | | 22 |

(at end of payroll)

*Total*

| —— | —— | —— | —— | —— | —— | —— | —— | —— | —— | —— | |

*Total Coinage Analysis*

| | | £5 | £1 | 50p | 10p | 5p | Copper | | | | |
|---|---|---|---|---|---|---|---|---|---|---|---|

# APPENDIX 2.4

PAYROLL

S/A................          Weekly          Date................

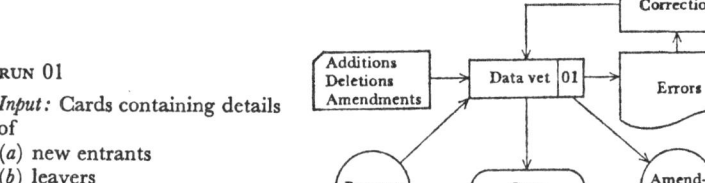

RUN 01

*Input:* Cards containing details of
(a) new entrants
(b) leavers
(c) changes in:
   (1) employee records
   (2) job number.

*Process:* Data vet and transcribe to magnetic tape.
Valuation checks:
(a) Mod. 11 check digit to:
   (1) employee number
   (2) current job number
   (3) new job number
(b) format check on 'name' field
(c) range check on
   (1) hourly rate field
   (2) N.I. rate field.

*Output:* Valid additions, deletions, amendments to magnetic tape; errors printed, corrections punched and verified to cards and re-input. Run not completed until all input correct.

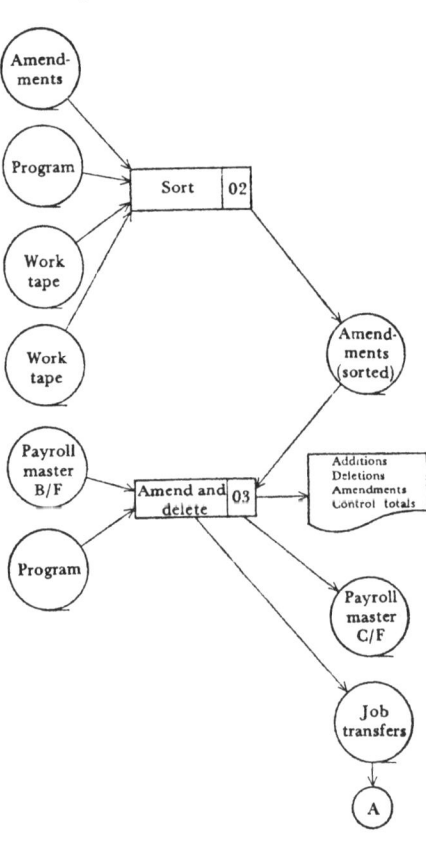

RUN 02

Amendments File sorted to
employee number sequence
within previous job number
sequence.

RUN 03

(1) Additions: inserted in
correct sequence on
Master File and written
to C/F File. Full record
printed.
(2) Deletions: record deleted
from Master File and
full record printed.
(3) Amendments: employee
record amended on
Master File and written
to C/F File.
(4) Transfers: employee
record written to Job
Transfer File and
deleted from Master File.
Employee record to be
printed for both (3) and
(4).
(5) Hash control totals
printed on employee
number.

56

S/A..................        Weekly        Date..................

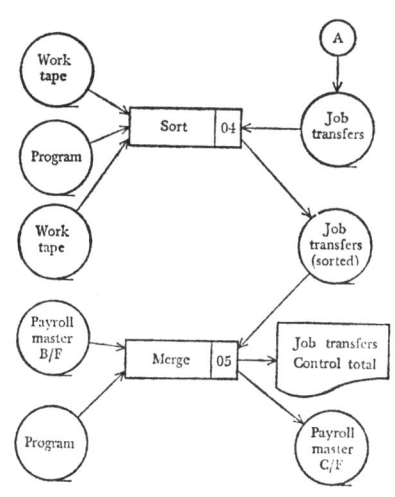

RUN 04

Job Transfer File sorted to
employee number sequence
and to new job number
sequence.

RUN 05

*Merge* employee records from
Job Transfer File to correct
sequence on Master File.

*Print* list of job transfers by
new job number, and hash
control total by new job
number.

RUN 06

*Input:* Punched cards.

*Process:* Data vet and transcribe to magnetic tape. Validation checks:
(*a*) modulus 11 check digit to:
   (1) employee number
   (2) current job number
(*b*) range check to:
   hours–normal
       –o/time (n)
       –o/time (s).

*Output*
(1) Valid data to Time Sheet Data File
(2) invalid data printed, corrected and re-input
(3) run not completed until all input correct.

RUN 07

*Sort* time sheet data to employee number sequence within current job number sequence.

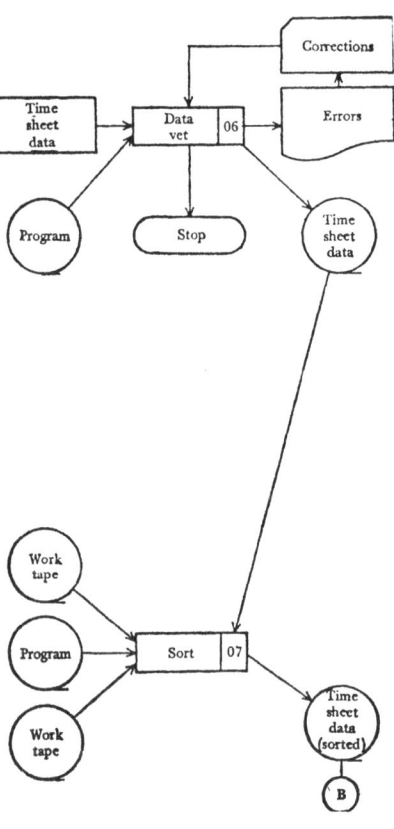

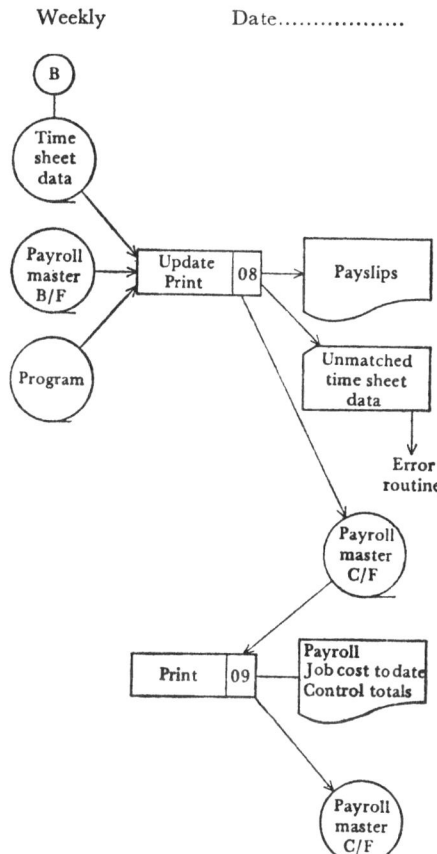

RUN 08

Time sheet data records matched with records on Payroll Master by employee number and job number.

*Match:* Calculate pay, update employee record and write to Master C/F Tape accumulate table by trade by job in store. Read job cost record from master at end of each job record, update and write to new Master.

*Mismatch:* Punch card with details of time sheet data—to error routine—manual calculation of pay.

RUN 09

*Rewind* tape.

*Read* Payroll Master.

*Print* Payroll, Coinage Analysis and Labour Job Cost by trade and total within job. Print payroll totals.

# RANDOM INTERROGATION OF A LARGE FILE

An approach to the problem outlined in the case study is first to determine the required outputs from the system.

These are stated on pp. 20–1 above as follows:

1. Cash Received book – daily.
2. Listing of accounts in arrear and arrears paid for head office – daily.
3. Listing of accounts in arrear and arrears paid for each branch – daily.
4. An interrogation system for ascertaining the current position of each account to be available to head office and to the branches.

Students having a reasonable understanding of E.D.P. systems will appreciate that outputs 1–3 present no particular problem. Output 4, however, requires some thought.

The alternatives are stated on p. 18: let us consider them in turn.

## PROCESSING IN REAL-TIME

This would be an ideal solution but is ruled out by cost. It would require a powerful machine, effectively in duplicate, with an expensive data terminal network, connecting each of the branches to the computer. So we are forced back to:

## BATCH PROCESSING

There are three alternatives:

(a) The use of an interrogating typewriter to interrupt the main program and deal with inquiries. To be really effective, this would mean an interrogating typewriter in each branch with, again, the expense of a data communications network. Alternatively we could have just one interrogating typewriter at head office and branches could phone in their inquiries.

What are the disadvantages of such a system?

1. Cost of hardware – such a system presupposes a direct-access storage device, a magnetic disc or drum.

2. The interrupt feature is very expensive of computer time and will slow down the main run considerably. This is another way of saying that we must invest more in the hardware to achieve the same objective.
3. A small point perhaps, but think of the client waiting in the branch for a clerk to telephone head office, contact the person on the interrogating typewriter, and wait for the reply. To be sure of a quick response it would be advisable to install a private telephone line to each branch. We are back at cost again.
4. Telephone messages can be misunderstood, particularly if there is noise on the line.

(*b*) So let us consider batching the inquiries. This will certainly reduce cost; we could indeed possibly dispense with a direct-access storage device. But consider the delay: inquiries are received at head office by post or telephone, punched in cards or paper tape, verified, processed, and replies communicated to the branch. This will certainly not be 'short-notice'; indeed the minimum time would probably be in the order of half a day. We can rule this out as it does not satisfy the requirements of management.

(*c*) So we are left with the last possibility – a complete historical print-out of the file. Daily? Weekly? Monthly? To be absolutely sure of having the current position of each account, we *must* print-out daily. Can we face a print-out of 200,000 accounts daily? Assuming that each account will occupy two lines of print, this makes 400,000 lines of print. Using a high-speed line printer running at 1,000 lines per minute, and allowing for paper throw and set-up time, we have approximately eight hours.

Can we overcome this impasse by printing out only details of accounts that have moved? If we assume twenty working days in the month and again two lines per account, then we are now faced with printing approximately 20,000 lines per day. On a fast line printer (1,000 lines per minute) this will take thirty minutes. If we use a much slower and cheaper printer, say 250 lines per minute, it will still take approximately only four hours.

If this method is used, it will be necessary, however, to

61

produce a daily index so that clerks have a quick means of referring to the appropriate day's print-out, which contains the up-to-date position of the account.

The solution adopted by this company was to allot to each day of the monthly processing cycle an alphabetical character; this caters for up to twenty-six days. Every day an index is produced, which shows the day on which the last account moved:

First, a heading is printed which is for one hundred vertical lines on the paper.

Heading   00000000001111111111--------9999999999

      0123456789012345678 9--------0123456789

Account No.

  0  -MBQCFQDEGHA-QFC-QHI

  1  FG-AFQQ-HGFBA-QHF-QF

The first line refers to accounts numbered 0–99, the second line to accounts numbered 100–199. Thus, account numbered 19 last moved on day I, and accounts numbered 102, 107, 113 and 117 are not in use. A straight listing of 200,000 accounts at 1,000 lines per minute would take about two minutes, at 250 lines per minute approximately eight minutes.

THE CONFIGURATION OF MACHINE REQUIRED

This requires the drafting of a computer flowchart, showing the peripherals used on each run. The system used and the configuration of machine required is shown on the following flowchart (Appendix 3.1).

The maximum number of tape decks used was five; in fact they had six as it is always advisable to have a spare to allow for possible breakdown of equipment.

The line printer operated at a rated speed of 600 lines per minute. A slower line printer would have completed the job in the time, but the faster printer, although more expensive, was chosen to provide a degree of flexibility.

Cash returns were collected from the branches twice daily by messenger, the cash records being punched and verified at head office and processed twice daily to build up the Index tape. The print-out of the Index, and the branch lists of accounts in arrear and paid, were dispatched to branches overnight.

The tape decks were utilised to their maximum, e.g. the Index was output from Store to tape as each line of print was assembled. This minimised the size of the core store, a very expensive form of hardware.

CONCLUSION

It is hoped that the reader of this case study will have devoted some time to developing possible solutions to the problem. In this event, the outcome should be the point that an information-retrieval system can be designed to meet management's requirements without the need to invest in expensive, sophisticated hardware. The system as installed can be improved upon in the light of more recent developments in systems and hardware. See if you can design an improved system.

# APPENDIX 3.1

HIRE-PURCHASE ACCOUNTING

S/A.................                  Daily                 Date.................

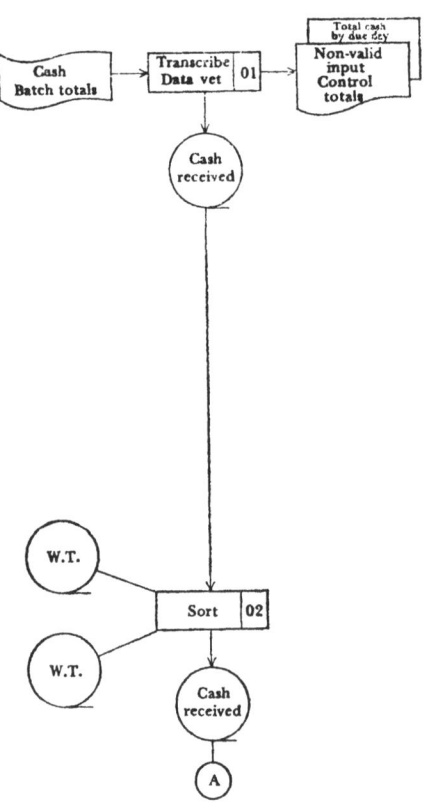

RUN 01

*Input*: Cash records with batch totals.

*Agree* date and batch number within each batch.

*Validate* account number by check digit.

*Agree* cash totals per batch with control totals.

*Output:* Printer.
Control totals discrepancies.
Non-valid input.
Total cash by due day and store—Mag. Tape
Valid cash receipts
(due day, account number, branch number, first four characters of surname, date, amount).

RUN 02

*Sort* to account number sequence.

S/A.................         Daily        Date.................

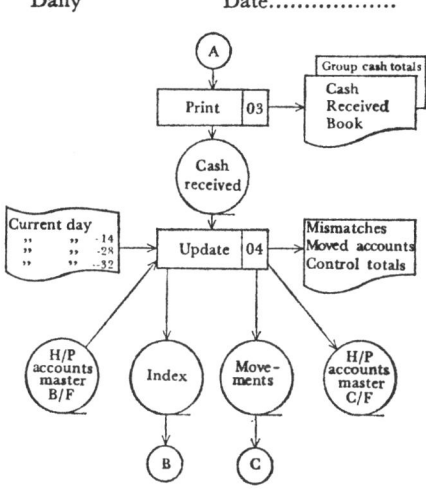

**RUN 03**

*Print* listing (Cash Book).
Accumulate cash totals for
each 10,000 account numbers.
Store and print group totals.

**RUN 04**

(1) *Read* alpha character
represents current day.

(2) *Read* block from H/P
Accounts Master B/F file.

   *Check* due day of record.

   *If* for current day:

   *Deduct* instalment from
balance.

   *Add* instalment to arrears.

   *Deduct* 1 from remaining
number of instalments.

   *Calculate* settlement =

$$\text{Balance} - \frac{\text{charges} \times \text{number of O/S instalments}}{\text{total number of instalments}}$$

(3) *Read* block from cash
received file.

   *Match* cash record with
accounts record on
account number.

   *Match* found.

   *Match* first four characters
of surname.

   *Mismatch:* Print
cash record in full.

   *Match:* Deduct cash from
'arrears'.
Insert current day
character in 'day last
moved' field.

   *Test:* 'Balance' and arrears

zero, add 'fully paid' to
record.

*Test:* 'Arrears'—if negative
and amount greater than
'balance' add 'overpaid' to
record.

*Print* and *Write* to
'movements' tape, details
of record:
Account number
Branch number
Transaction type (2 for
cash)
Due day (alpha char.)
Amount paid
Present arrears
Overdue designation
Fully paid
Overpaid.

(4) *All other account records*

*Test* 'due day' against
'day—14'.

*If* equality, insert 1 in
'overdue designation'.

*If* 'overdue designation'
= 3, insert 4 = 46 days
'overdue designation'.

*Test* 'due-day' against
'day—28'.

*If* equality, insert 2 in
'overdue designation'.

*Test* 'due-day' against
'day—32'.

*If* equality, insert 3 in
'overdue designation'.

*If* 'overdue designation'
changed, *insert* character
for current day in 'day
last moved' field.

*Print* and *Write* to
'movements'
tape details of record:
Account number
Branch number

S/A..................          Daily          Date..................

Transaction type (1 for
arrears)
Due day
Balance
Arrears
Overdue designation
Monthly instalments
Name and address.

(5) *For all records*

Written to 'movements'
tape.

*Write* 'day last moved'
character from record to
the appropriate position
in store. As each index
print line is completed,
it is written to the 'index'
tape.

*Accumulate* totals of cash,
arrears and balances.

*Print* totals for each group
of 10,000 accounts.

*Print* any discrepancies
with cash totals accumu-
lated in Run 03.

*Write* block of updated
accounts records to Hire-
Purchase Accounts Master
C/F file.

67

S/A...................                    Daily                    Date..................

**RUN** 05

*Print* Index. Where no account exists for an account number, a dash (-) is inserted.

**RUN** 06

*Print* accounts in arrear and paid.

**RUN** 07

*Sort* movements file to branch sequence.

**RUN** 08

*Print* lists of accounts in arrear and paid.
New page for each branch.

## PRODUCTION SCHEDULING

The usual approach to a solution is to commence with the required outputs, and work back to inputs, files and processing. In this case study, however, the student should consider firstly the question of data capture. Approximately 100 van-men arrive between 3.30 p.m. and 4 p.m. to place their orders, all of which, together with the parcels orders, must be processed between 4 p.m. and 5 p.m. This rules out the more usual methods of data capture, e.g. punched cards or punched paper tape. One solution which springs to mind is to use mark-sensed cards; however, as the van-men are already familiar with the use of pre-printed order forms, the student should take advantage of this and use a pre-printed order form designed to be marked by the van-men and read through an optical mark reader. An outline of a form is shown (Appendix 4.1). Four form types will be printed, each type being designated by a pre-printed mark on the line 'Form Type', as follows:

(a) First mark. Van orders Bread – two sheets marked sheets 1 and 2.
(b) Second mark. Van orders Confectionery – three sheets marked sheets 1, 2 and 3.
(c) Third mark. Parcels amendment orders Bread – two sheets marked 1 and 2.
(d) Fourth mark. Parcels amendment orders Confectionery – three sheets marked 1, 2 and 3.

Amendments received from parcels customers will be marked up on the sheets by clerks in the office. Van-men will mark up sheets as they arrive in the office placing their orders for bread for delivery next day and for confectionery to be baked the next day for delivery the following day. This will result in 750 order sheets plus 75 (5 per cent of 1,500) from parcels customers, which can be read into the computer by an optical mark reader in five and a half minutes.

The student is now advised to concentrate on the design of the required outputs and the necessary files. The invoice for the parcels customers (see Appendix 4.2) should not present any problem. The file to support the parcels customers is probably

69

best held on two files, one to hold sales ledger data, the other holding the standing orders for each day of the week, with a summary at the end of each day's records of the production requirements (see Appendix 4.3).

The output for the van-men must provide the details of the products supplied to them each day, together with a daily statement of their account with the company (see Appendix 4.4). The van-men's master file is very simple (see Appendix 4.3). In order to shorten these files, a product file containing information such as alphabetical descriptions, prices, etc., is held on magnetic tape (see Appendix 4.3). This is a very short file which can be held in the memory of the machine, thus minimising on sorting.

Having designed the input, outputs and files, and bearing in mind that you may have to go back and amend these designs, all that remains is to draw up computer flowcharts for the processing of the data (see Appendix 4.6).

The method adopted was to amend the Product file as necessary and read the file into memory. A print-out of the amendments was made as a routine check, and the amended file written to magnetic tape for use the next day (Run 01). The amendments to the standing orders of parcels customers are then read in through the mark reader, validated, corrected and written to magnetic tape (Run 02). This tape is sorted to customer number order, and run against the Standing Orders file and the Parcels Customer master file. Standing Orders are amended by the Amendments file, the orders are extended by reference to the Product file held in memory; invoices and delivery notes are printed, the Customer master file is updated and written to magnetic tape. The Standing Orders file is written to magnetic tape after amendment where amendments are designated Permanent. All amendments for the day are accumulated in store by product; at the end of the run the production summary for the day is read, amended and written to magnetic tape (Run 04). The production requirements are then sorted to products code sequence (Run 05). These five runs can be completed before 4 p.m.

As the van-men come into the office they will complete their order forms by marking their requirements for bread to be loaded the next morning, and for confectionery to be baked the next day. On the completion of these order forms, they will be read through the optical mark reader, validated, corrected, and written to magnetic tape (Run 06). The next run is to sort the orders to van number sequence within product code sequence (Run 07). On Run 08 the bread baked on that day's shift which is surplus to requirements is read in using the paper-tape reader and held in store. The Product Requirements file for the parcels customers, from Run 05, is loaded on to a tape deck. The processing then is to read orders for bread (coded 01–70) from the van Orders file and build up production requirements for the night shift by product, by load bay, to print out the production schedule (see Appendix 4.5); at the same time the orders are extended by reference to the Product file, still held in store, and then written to magnetic tape. The production requirements for the day shift can now be produced (see Appendix 4.5) by first reading, accumulating and printing the bread orders from the Product Requirements (Parcels) file, followed by the confectionery requirements from both the Product Requirements (Parcels) file and the van-men's Orders file. Van-men's orders for confectionery are extended and written to the Extended Orders file. All Product Requirements are written to a Total Product Requirements file, which will now contain bread requirements for the night shift, followed by bread and confectionery requirements for the day shift. In Run 09 a Product Specification file is loaded into store, and the Total Product Requirements file is extended to provide the Raw Materials Requirement for each quantity of each product to be manufactured.

This Raw Materials file is sorted on the Raw Materials code, in two sorts, the first sort being the Raw Materials for the van-men's orders for bread, which is written to one tape deck (night shift), the second sort being on the remainder of the file and written to a second tape deck (day shift), Run 10. In Run 11 the Raw Materials Requirements (night shift) is run against the Raw Materials Stock master file, which is updated, and a print-out of Raw Materials required for the night shift is made. In the next run (Run 12) the same process is repeated for the Raw Materials Requirement for the day shift, this being followed by a print-out of a Stock Report. The final three runs (Runs 13, 14 and 15) are straightforward. Cash and Returns punched into paper tape are validated, written to magnetic tape, then together with the Extended Orders file from Run 08 they are sorted to van-number order, and run with the Van-men's master file to prepare the Van Order Sheets and Statements of Accounts, and to update the Van-men's master file.

When calculating the total time, one must appreciate that the critical timing period does not start until Run 06. The approximate time for the last ten runs is as follows:

|  |  | *Mins* |
|---|---|---|
| *Run 06* | Read 750 documents through U.D.T. at 150 per minute | 5·00 |
|  | Set up and correction, say | 5·00 |
| *Run 07* | Sort 150 × 70 records, say | 2·00 |

*Run 08*  Print production schedules

| | | |
|---|---|---|
| Bread night shift, say | 80 lines | |
| Bread day shift, say | 80 lines | |
| Confectionery day shift, say | 110 lines | |
| | —— | |
| | 270 lines | |

| | | |
|---|---|---|
| at 600 l.p.m., say | | 0·50 |

Write Total Production Requirements file

| | | |
|---|---|---|
| Van orders | 150 × 70 = 10,500 records | |
| Parcel | 300 × 12 = 3,600 records | |
| | —————— | |
| | 14,100 records | |

14,100 records × 8 characters
= 112,800 characters at 20·8 Kc. = 5 secs.
∴ Printing will take longer
Set-up time: paper-tape reader
     3 tape decks
     Printer  say         5·00

*Run 09*  Read Total Production Requirements file
      *see above* 5 secs.
Read Product Specifications file, negligible
Set-up 1 tape deck
    Total time including rewind, say   2·00

|  |  | *Mins* |
|---|---|---|
| *Run 10* | Sort Raw Materials file | 1·00 |
| *Run 11* | Print Raw Materials night shift, say | 1·00 |
| *Run 12* | Print Raw Materials day shift, say | 1·00 |
|  | Set-up and rewind time, say | 2·00 |

*Run 13*   Read paper tape

             150 van-men with one cash record each

             of (Date 6 chars. Cash 5 chars.)

             $= 150 \times 11$ characters $= 1{,}650$

             at 1,000 chars./sec. $= 1·65$ secs

             Returns, say       0·35 secs

                        2·00 secs        0·03

     Set-up time                               1·00

*Run 14*   Sort                                            1·00

*Run 15*   Print Van Order sheets

             Average      70 lines

             Header        3 lines

             Statement    6 lines

             Spaces        6 lines

                       85 lines

     150 Order sheets $= 12{,}700$ lines at 600 l.p.m.      22·00

     Set-up time                                5·00

                                        53·53

The job can be done between 4 p.m. and 5 p.m.

ORDER – VAN No.

BREAD

(35 orders per sheet)

| Description | Selling price | Unit qty. | Product code | Form type Parcels Perm/Temp Van/Cust Number Quantity | | P | T | | | | Sheet Number | | | |
|---|---|---|---|---|---|---|---|---|---|---|---|---|---|---|
| | | | | | | 100 – 200 | 10 | 20 | 40 | 80 | 1 | 2 | 3 – 4 | 4 – 8 |
| Farmhouse Lge | | Sgl | 003 | | | 100 – 200 | 10 | 20 | 40 | 80 | 1 | 2 | 4 | 8 |
| Farmhouse Sml | | Sgl | 004 | | | 100 – 200 | 10 | 20 | 40 | 80 | 1 | 2 | 4 | 8 |
| Sandwich Lge | | Sgl | 005 | | | 100 – 200 | 10 | 20 | 40 | 80 | 1 | 2 | 4 | 8 |
| Sandwich Sml | | Sgl | 009 | | | 100 – 200 | 10 | 20 | 40 | 80 | 1 | 2 | 4 | 8 |
| Danish Lge | | Sgl | 006 | | | 100 – 200 | 10 | 20 | 40 | 80 | 1 | 2 | 4 | 8 |
| Danish Sml | | Sgl | 007 | | | 100 – 200 | 10 | 20 | 40 | 80 | 1 | 2 | 4 | 8 |
| Rolls Crisp | | Doz | 008 | | | 100 – 200 | 10 | 20 | 40 | 80 | 1 | 2 | 4 | 8 |
| | | | | | | 100 – 200 | 10 | 20 | 40 | 80 | 1 | 2 | 4 | 8 |
| | | | | | | 100 – 200 | 10 | 20 | 40 | 80 | 1 | 2 | 4 | 8 |
| | | | | | | 100 – 200 | 10 | 20 | 40 | 80 | 1 | 2 | 4 | 8 |

# APPENDIX 4.2

## PARCELS INVOICE

JOHN SMITH & SONS
THE MARKET
NORMCESTER
LINCS.

BURKE BAKERIES LTD
HIGH ROAD
SLUB TOWN
WORCS.

| Invoice No. 1234 | Date 18.02.71 | | | Route 9.55 Birmingham | |
|---|---|---|---|---|---|
| Description | Commodity code | Unit Qty | Qty | Price | Value |
| Farmhouse    large | 003 | SGL | 20 | | |
| W'meal        small | 015 | SGL | 10 | | |
| Bath buns | 114 | DOZ | 5 | | |
| Jam tarts    boxes 6 | 127 | SGL | 9 | | |
| Cream sponge | 142 | SGL | 12 | | |
| Swiss roll – jam | 153 | SGL | 18 | | |

FILE RECORDS – MAGNETIC TAPE

PARCELS CUSTOMERS – STANDING ORDERS FILE

| | Cust. No. | Day | Comm code | Qty | Comm code | Qty | Comm code | Qty | Summary of product requirements by product for each day at end of file |
|---|---|---|---|---|---|---|---|---|---|
| No. of words | 1 | 1 | 1 | 1 | 1 | 1 | 1 | 1 | |

Average 12 records/customer →

Five blocks per customer →

PARCELS CUSTOMERS – MASTER FILE

| | Cust. No. | N/A | Route | Opening balance | Inv. No. | Date | Amount | | Cash ref. | Date | Amount |
|---|---|---|---|---|---|---|---|---|---|---|---|
| No. of words | 1 | 25 | 5 | 2 | 2 | 2 | 1 | – – – – – | 2 | 2 | 1 |

PRODUCT FILE

| Comm code | Description | Unit code | Unit price | Comm code | Description | Unit code | Unit price | Comm code | Desc. |
|---|---|---|---|---|---|---|---|---|---|
| 1 | 6 | 1 | 1 | 1 | 6 | 1 | 1 | 1 | |

No. of words

Each product = 9 words;  170 products = 1,530 words.

VAN-MEN – MASTER FILE

| Van No. | Name | Date | Current balance | Total sales to date for month |
|---|---|---|---|---|
| 1 | 5 | 2 | 2 | 2 |

No. of words

# APPENDIX 4.4

## DETAIL ORDER SHEET – VAN

| Van No. 043 | Bay No. 2 | Name F. Brown | Date 18·02·71 |
|---|---|---|---|

| Commodity – Bread | | Code | Unit Qty | Qty | Price | Value |
|---|---|---|---|---|---|---|
| Farmhouse | Lge | 003 | SGL | 42 | | |
| Farmhouse | Sml | 004 | SGL | 48 | | |
| W'meal | Lge | 014 | SGL | 36 | | |
| W'meal | Sml | 015 | SGL | 54 | | |
| Rolls | C'tail | 048 | DOZ | 8 | | |

| Van No. 043 | Bay No. 2 | Name F. Brown | Date 18.02.71 |
|---|---|---|---|

| Commodity – Confy | Code | Unit Qty | Qty | Price | Value |
|---|---|---|---|---|---|
| Bath buns | 114 | DOZ | 6 | | |
| Cream sponge | 142 | SGL | 24 | | |
| Swiss roll – jam | 153 | SGL | 25 | | |

| Van No. 043 | Bay No. 2 | Name F. Brown | Date 18.02.71 |
|---|---|---|---|

| Details | Debit | Credit | Balance |
|---|---|---|---|
| Balance     b/forward | | | 42·50 |
| Bread | | | |
| Confectionery | | | |
| Cash | | 42·00 | |
| Returns | | 00·50 | |
| Balance     due | | | |

## APPENDIX 4.5

### BREAD REQUIREMENTS (VAN)

| Commodity | | Quantity | | | | | Total del. | Day shift prod. | Night shift prod. |
|---|---|---|---|---|---|---|---|---|---|
| | | Bay 1 | Bay 2 | Bay 3 | Bay 4 | Bay 5 | | | |
| Farmhouse | Lge | 300 | 142 | 156 | 174 | 241 | 1,013 | 150 | 863 |
| Farmhouse | Sml | 206 | 231 | 193 | 165 | 270 | 1,065 | 210 | 855 |
| W'meal | Lge | 97 | 86 | 102 | 79 | 89 | 453 | — | 453 |
| W'meal | Sml | 102 | 171 | 152 | 193 | 147 | 765 | — | 765 |
| Hovis | Sml | 89 | 111 | 93 | -21 | 78 | 492 | — | 492 |

### BREAD REQUIREMENTS (PARCELS)

| Commodity | | Qty |
|---|---|---|
| Farmhouse | Lge | 141 |
| Farmhouse | Sml | 206 |
| W'meal | Lge | 191 |
| W'meal | Sml | 173 |
| Hovis | Sml | 97 |

CONFECTIONERY REQUIREMENTS

| Commodity | Quantity | | | | | | |
|---|---|---|---|---|---|---|---|
| | Bay 1 | Bay 2 | Bay 3 | Bay 4 | Bay 5 | Parcels | Total |
| Bath buns | 49 | 72 | 102 | 48 | 51 | 149 | 471 |
| Cream sponge | 24 | 36 | 48 | 12 | 30 | 72 | 222 |
| Swiss roll – jam | 48 | 54 | 36 | 42 | 30 | 96 | 306 |

# APPENDIX 4.6

PRODUCTION SCHEDULING

S/A.................                Daily                Date.................

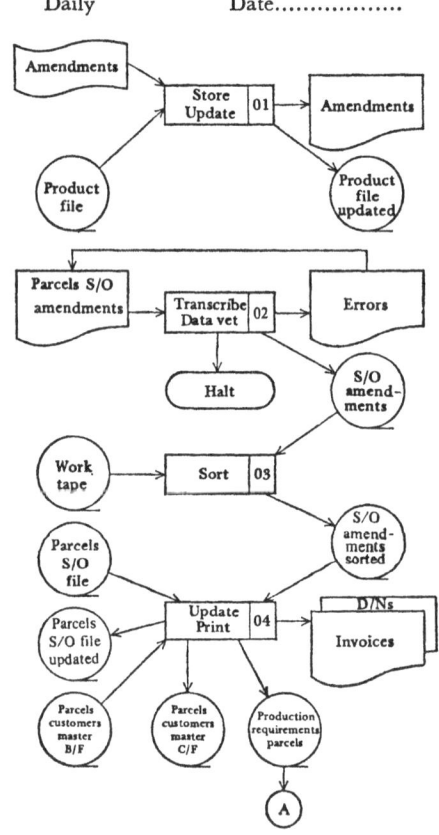

**RUN 01**

*Read* Product File and Store.

*Read* Amendments tape, amend file in Store.

*Write* updated Product File.

**RUN 02**

*Read* standing orders amendments through U.D.T.

*Validate,* correct errors.

*Write* to mag. tape.

**RUN 03**

*Sort* standing orders amendments to customer number order.

**RUN 04**

*Read* parcels customer master.

*Print* N/A, route, inv. no. and date.

*Read* Standing Orders File for relevant customer and day.

*Read* Standing Orders Amendment File.

*Amend* standing order as necessary.

*Price and extend* order from Product File held in Store.

*Print* invoice line.

*Accumulate* amendments in Store by product.

*At end* of Standing Orders File *read* day's production requirements.

S/A.................                    Daily                    Date.................

*Amend* by accumulated
amendments.

*Write* production requirements
to mag. tape.

RUN 05

Sort to commodity code
order

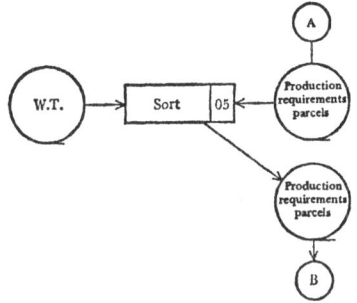

RUN 06

*Read* van orders through
U.D.T. *Validate* input.
Correct errors.

*Write* to mag. tape.

RUN 07

*Sort* to van no. order within
commodity code order.

RUN 08

*Read* surplus bread production
on day shift and store.

*Read* Van Orders File
commodities 01–70. Accumulate by commodity by load
bay and by total. (Load bay 1
=vans No. 1–30 etc.)

*Deduct* surplus bread where
applicable.

*Print* production requirements for night shift.

*Write* to mag. tape
*Extend* orders by ref. to
Product File.

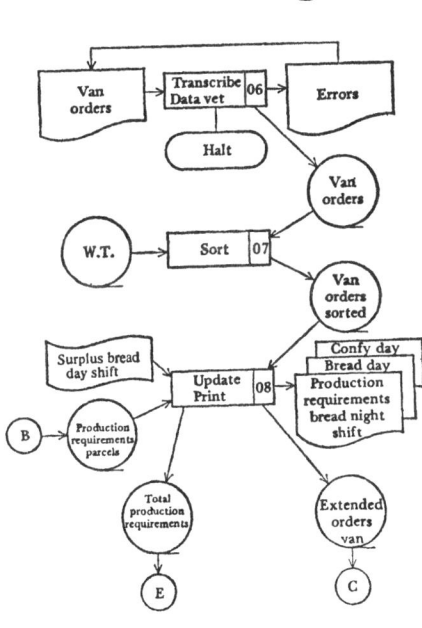

S/A................              Daily              Date.................

*Write* to Extended Orders
Tape.

*Read* production requirements
parcels commodities 01–70.

*Accumulate* by commodity.

*Print* production requirements
bread day shift.

*Write* to mag. tape.

*Read* Van Orders File.

*Read* Production Requirements Parcels File.

*Accumulate* by commodity by
load bay and parcels and by
total.

*Print* production requiremen's
confectionery.

*Write* to mag. tape.

*Extend* van orders by ref. to
Product File.

*Write* to Extended Orders
Tape.

RUN 09

*Read* Product Specifications
File to Store.

*Read* Product Requirements
File. Multiply quantity by
raw materials in Product
Spec. File.

*Write* extended production
requirements.

RUN 10

*Sort* on raw material code.

*Write* R.M. requirements
(night shift) to mag. tape.

*Write* R.M. requirements
(day shift) to mag. tape.

RUN 11

*Update* Stock Master by R.M.
requirements (night shift)

*Acc.* by R.M. code.

*Print* R.M. (night shift).

RUN 12

*Rewind* Stock Master.

*Update* Stock Master by
R.M. requirements.

*Acc.* by R.M. code.

*Print* R.M. (day shift).

*Print* Stock report.

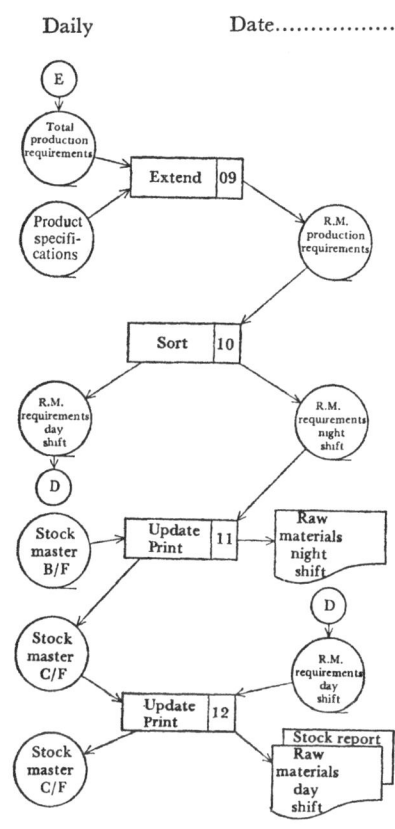

S/A................       Daily       Date................

RUN 13

*Read* Cash and returns from P.P.T.

*Validate* and *Write* to mag. tape.

RUN 14

*Sort* to van number order.

RUN 15

*Update* Van Master File by Extended Orders File and Cash Returns File.

*Print* detailed order sheets and statement of account for van-men.

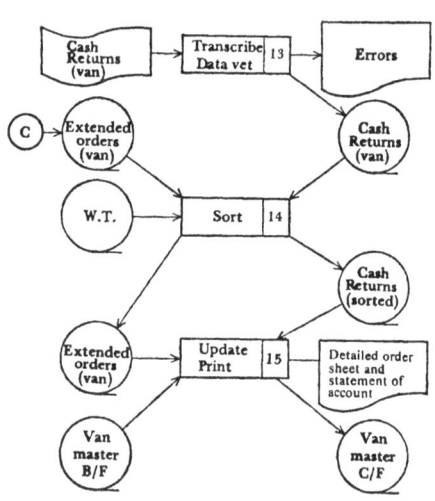

# INTEGRATED DATA PROCESSING

The approach to the case study should be first to list down clearly the principal outputs required both daily and monthly. These are invoices and statements, the statistics required being normally in tabular form, although we should consider the possibility of producing the sales per customer by commodity in the same run as the statements. Design a form for the invoice, bearing in mind the need to reduce print lines and paper throws as far as possible, without destroying the appearance of the form. Compare your design with that shown in Appendix 5.1.

Now design the statement, a much simpler form, then compare your design with that shown in Appendix 5.2; note that the production of sales statistics per customer by commodity can be printed in the same run as the statements, either as shown as part of the statement but removed later by perforation or cutting, or printed as a separate tabulation but side by side with the statement.

Having considered the main outputs, it is now possible to proceed to the needs of inputs. These are in punched-card form and it will be necessary to prepare outline designs for these cards. When undertaking this task it is as well to keep in mind the data which you will wish to keep on the files. Broadly the punched-card inputs will contain:

(a) Reference data – i.e. the necessary link to a file record, e.g. a customer number.
(b) Variable data – i.e. the data which cannot be predetermined, e.g. quantity ordered.

All other data should be written to a file.

There are two items of variable data to be input:

(a) Details of orders from customers.
(b) Details of changes, additions, deletions, amendments to the stock of patterns and to the Customer file.

Prepare card designs for these two inputs and compare them with the card designs in Appendices 5.3 and 5.4. Note that with a computer a 'spread' card can be used, i.e. it is not necessary to restrict each card to one transaction. If we keep the Stock file on the disc, then the sales order card can accommodate three order items, and the Stock file can be accessed randomly. This reduces card consumption and speeds up the card-read time.

Now it is necessary to prepare file record layouts. To do this you must have in mind the broad basis on which you intend to process, so draw up a computer flowchart in the rough, leaving the detailed flowchart to the end. It will soon become clear that the sales ledger (Customer master file) will have to be held on magnetic tape, and furthermore that there will be considerable advantages, in the saving of sort runs, if we can hold the Stock file on the disc. It will then be possible to batch process orders and the Customer file together, having previously sorted the orders to the same sequence, and during the same run access the Stock file which, although in a different sequence, can be accessed randomly either by an index held on the disc or by a generated address. If we include in the customer record the area number allocated to the customer, it will be possible to build up on the disc a table of sales statistics by area. You will find that you will be repeatedly changing and amending firstly your rough flowchart and then your file layouts, a to-and-fro process which is quite time-consuming but unavoidable. When you are satisfied with your result, then refer to Appendices 5.5 to 5.7. The important thing is to see where your solution differs from the model solution. There is no best answer, and several good solutions are possible.

I shall now take you through the solution presented:

The Stock file is held on disc (see Appendix 5.5); each record is 32 characters in length so that 100 records can be held per track and the Stock file of 5,000 items will occupy 5 cylinders.

The Sales Analysis by Area table held on disc (see Appendix 5.5) is 363 characters in length. Nine records can be held on a track and therefore 400 records will occupy 4·5 cylinders. As there are 200 cylinders on the disc store, it would appear feasible to hold the suite of programs on the disc as well.

The customer record (see Appendix 5.6) consists of a fixed-length record of 365 characters, including the sales analysis by commodity per customer; followed by a variable length record, detailing invoices raised and cash items received during the month. The operating system supplied with the machine will handle variable-length records quite easily, and will also deal with the unblocking and reblocking of records on magnetic tape.

There are four daily runs (see Appendix 5.7). Run 01 is to amend the Stock file for additions, deletions and for price changes, parameter changes, etc. Any errors detected on input will have to be corrected and re-input before Run 02, when current and outstanding orders are checked against the stock availability, and where stock is available valid extended orders are output to magnetic tape, and the Stock file updated. Where no stock is available, the orders are output to the Outstanding Orders file. Cash received and amendments to the Customer master file are validated and written to the Valid Orders file. Run 03 is a sort of Valid Orders, etc., file to customer-number order. Run 04, the main run, updates the Customer master file firstly for amendments, secondly for valid orders, thirdly for cash received, and lastly updates the sales analysis record. The updated record is written to the new Customer master file, and an invoice is printed. The sales analysis table on the disc is updated, and at the end of the run a print-out of the value of sales by area is made from this table.

The four monthly runs are concerned with the production of statements and sales statistics. Run 11 is a straight print-out of customers' statements and sales analysis by commodity per customer from the records on the Customer master file. The variable-length record on the Customer master file is deleted and the new balance written to the updated file. A copy of the statement is filed as an historical record of the account.

Run 12 is a print-out from the sales analysis table on the disc of sales by commodity by area. A copy of this tabulation also serves as a tabulation of sales by area for the month to enable representatives' commission to be prepared.

In Run 13 the sales analysis table is scanned to print out a tabulation of sales by commodity by area. The last run is a management stock status report, used mainly for detecting slow-moving or obsolete patterns.

TIMING

To time the runs, in theory one should time each peripheral, the disc and the processor. Then, as all peripherals are buffered, the time for the run will be the longest time taken by any one peripheral. In practice it is almost unheard of for a run to be 'process bound' on a data-processing application, owing to the speed of the C.P.U. in relation to the usage of the peripherals.

For example, in Run 01 the time of the run will clearly be limited by the speed at which the cards can be read as the line printer operates at a higher speed than the card reader.

DAILY RUNS

*Run 01*

If we assume a maximum of 10 per cent amendments to the Stock file, this will involve reading

> 500 cards at 600 cards per minute = say 1 minute
> Plus set-up time for card reader,
> > disc and printer      say 3 minutes
> >
> >      Total time     4 minutes

*Run 02*

  *Card reader*

Average 3,000 order cards at 600 c.p.m.      = 5·0 minutes
(up to 3 orders per card)
Average 1,500 cash cards at 600 c.p.m.      = 2·5 minutes
Average say 600 amendment cards at 600 c.p.m. = 1·0 minutes

                                             8·5 minutes

  *Magnetic tape*

Assume records unblocked when written to Valid Orders file. Characters to be written to tape:

| | | |
|---|---|---|
| Order records | $3,000 \times 78 =$ | $234,000$ |
| Cash records | $1,500 \times 27 =$ | $40,500$ |
| Amendment records | $300 \times 118 =$ | $35,400$ |
| | $4,800$ | $309,900$ |

Character time $\qquad \dfrac{309,900}{90,000} = 3\cdot4$ secs.

Gap time $\qquad \dfrac{4,800 \times 7}{1,000} = 33\cdot6$ secs.

$$\text{Total} = 37\cdot0 \text{ secs.}$$

In addition, the Outstanding Orders file has to be read and written, but the total time will not exceed the time for the card reader.

*Disc*

Average 3,000 invoices with average two items per invoice = 6,000 stock records to be accessed.

Character time $\qquad \dfrac{6,000 \times 32}{156,000} = 1\cdot2$ secs.

Latency time $\qquad \dfrac{6,000 \times 9}{1,000} = 54\cdot0$ secs.

Arm movement  Min. 12 m.s.
Over 5 cylinders  Max. 16 m.s.

Average $\qquad \dfrac{14 \text{ m.s.} \times 6,000}{1,000} = 84\cdot0$ secs.

Arm movement will normally take place outside of computer time. This run will be 'card reader limited'.

| | | |
|---|---|---|
| Run time | say | 9 minutes |
| Set-up time | | 6 minutes |
| Total time | | 15 minutes |

*Run 04*

*Magnetic tape*

Read Valid Orders, etc., file (see Run 02)    39·4 secs.

Read Customer master file.

To time this it is necessary to work out a blocking factor for the file. This is impossible until you can prepare a core map, showing the allocation of core store between program, working store, input and output areas. We can, however, work on some assumptions:

Core store $= 128$ K

Assume program, working store $= 80$ K

For input/output $= 48$ K

If we double buffer (useful as we have only two channels) then we need two input/output areas, therefore core available is 24 K, say 12 K for input and 12 K for output.

Now, how long is a customer record? Fixed length 365 characters, variable length say 125 characters, round it off to 500 characters. With input area of 12 K characters we could block at 24 records to the block – play it safe, make it 20.

$$\text{Character time} \quad \frac{60,000 \times 500}{90,000} = 333 \text{ secs.}$$

$$\text{Stop/start time} \quad \frac{60,000 \times 7}{20 \times 1,000} = 21 \text{ secs.}$$

As we are buffering in core, we can read from tape and write to tape at the same time.

Therefore total magnetic tape time $= 393$ seconds
$= 6·5$ minutes.

*Printer*

This time will be affected by the design of the invoice. The timing for the specimen in Appendix 5.1 is as follows:

| Line | Print lines | Spaces |
|---|---|---|
| Name and address | 4 | 1 |
| Account No. | 1 | 2 |
| Header | 1 | 3 |
| Body (average) | 2 | 1 |
| Total | 1 | |
| Discount | 1 | |
| Total | 1 | |
| Purchase tax | 1 | |
| Total | 1 | |
| Carriage | 1 | |
| Total | 1 | |
| To next name and address | | 3 |
| | 15 | 10 |

No long skips, therefore print time is

$$\frac{25}{1,200} \times 3,000 = 60\cdot25 \text{ minutes}$$

To this must be added the print time for sales per area = 400 lines + header.

$$\text{say} \quad \frac{405}{1,200} = 0\cdot3 \text{ minute}$$

This run is printer limited, time for the run being 60·55 minutes.

Set-up time (say)  5·00 minutes

Total time  (say)  66·00 minutes

TO SUMMATE

| | Minutes |
|---|---|
| Run 01 | 4 |
| Run 02 | 15 |
| Run 04 | 66 |
| | 85 |
| Sort time Run 03 say | 1 |
| | 86 |

Say 1½ hours per day.

*Run 11*

This run will be limited by the printer time, so let us not bother with other times.

*Printer*

Statements – as the sales by commodity by customer will be printed at the same time:

$$\begin{array}{ll} \text{Print lines} = & 20 \\ \text{Spaces} \quad\ \ = & 2 \\ \hline & 22 \end{array}$$

$$30{,}000 \text{ statements} = \frac{30{,}000}{1{,}200} \times 22 = 550 \text{ minutes.}$$

*Run 12*

Print sales by commodity within area.
Heading will be area. Print format as follows:

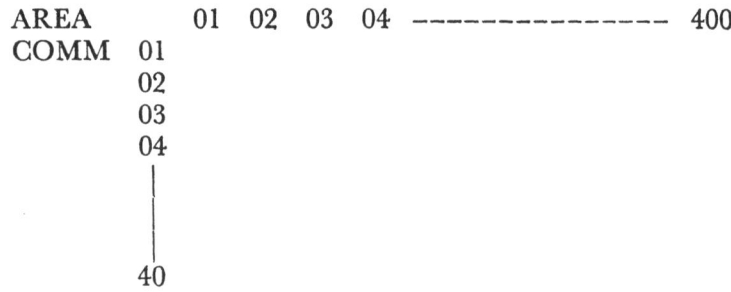

'COMM' = 7 print positions.

Allow 7 print positions + 1 space per area, we can get 14 areas across the page; therefore we shall need 29 pages.

$$\text{Each page} = 41 \text{ print lines plus say 4 spaces.}$$

$$\text{Print time} = \frac{29 \times 45}{1{,}200} = 1 \text{ minute.}$$

*Run 13*

Print format will be as follows:

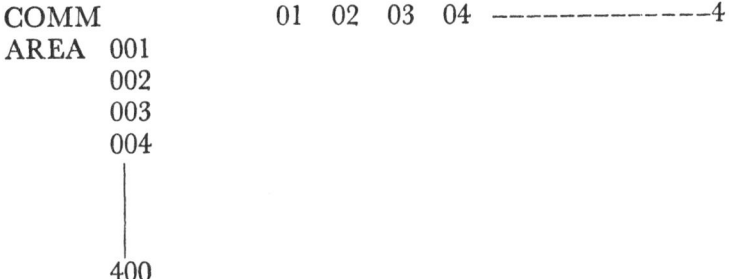

'AREA' = 8 print positions.

Allow 8 print positions per commodity = 14 commodities per page; therefore we shall print 3 pages.

Printer time: 400 lines plus say 4 spaces

$$\frac{404}{1,200} = 0.3 \text{ minute.}$$

*Run 14*

Printer time will depend on the number of stock items requiring to be reported; say 5 per cent fall into this category, the time will be

$$\frac{250}{1,200} = 0.5 \text{ minute.}$$

TO SUMMATE

|  |  | *Minutes* |
|---|---|---|
| Run | 11 | 550·0 |
|  | 12 | 1·0 |
|  | 13 | 0·3 |
|  | 14 | 0·5 |
|  |  | 551·8 |
|  | Set-up time (say) | 10·0 |
|  |  | 561·8 |

= 9 hours 21 minutes
say *9½ hours.*

As this time is so long, you may decide to recommend the partitioning of the monthly run and process, say, areas 1–200 on the 15th of the month and 201–400 on the 31st.

# APPENDIX 5.1

HOME LOVERS LTD     WALL COVERINGS LTD     *Invoice No.* 432645
14 NONSUCH ROAD         NEWTOWN
ANYTOWN               FARSHIRE
BLANKSHIRE

*Account No.* 59876734                        *Date* 14.11.70

| *Your order no.* 143261 | *Our order no.* 246832 | *Trade terms* 10% | | *Dispatch* Rail |
|---|---|---|---|---|
| *Pattern no.* | *Qty* | *Price* | *P/Tax* | *Value* | *Consignee* |
| 23/423160 | 10 | 07·50 | 00·75 | 75·00 | JONES FROME ST EXETER |
| | | | | 75·00 | |
| | | Discount | | 7·50 | |
| | | | | 67·50 | |
| | | P/Tax | | 7·50 | |
| | | | | 75·00 | |
| | | Carriage | | | |
| | | *Total* | | £ 75·00 | |

| | STATEMENT | | | | Sales/Commodity Cust. |
| --- | --- | --- | --- | --- | --- |

HOME LOVERS LTD   WALLCOVERINGS LTD
14 NONSUCH ROAD   NEWTOWN
ANYTOWN   FARSHIRE
BLANKSHIRE

*Account no.* 59876734          *Date* 30.11.70

| Date | Ref. no | Debit | Credit | Balance |
| --- | --- | --- | --- | --- |
| 01.11.70 | | | | 142·00 |
| 14.11.70 | 432645 | 75·00 | | |
| 25.11.70 | 573124 | 117·25 | | |
| 28.11.70 | 011436 | | 217·00 | |
| 30.11.70 | | | | 117·25 |
| | *Amount due* | | | £ 117·25 |

*Sales/Commodity Cust.*
*No.* 59876734

| | | | |
| --- | --- | --- | --- |
| 01 | | 21 | |
| 02 | | 22 | |
| 03 | | 23 | 75·00 |
| 04 | | 24 | |
| 05 | | 25 | |
| 06 | | 26 | |
| 07 | | 27 | |
| 08 | 117·25 | 28 | |
| 09 | | 29 | |
| 10 | | 30 | |
| 11 | | 31 | |
| 12 | | 32 | |
| 13 | | 33 | |
| 14 | | 34 | |
| 15 | | 35 | |
| 16 | | 36 | |
| 17 | | 37 | |
| 18 | | 38 | |
| 19 | | 39 | |
| 20 | | 40 | |

# APPENDIX 5.3

## STOCK AMENDMENT CARD

| | C A R D T Y P E | Commodity code and Pattern No. | Price | Qty | Min stock | Max stock | Date | DR or CR |
|---|---|---|---|---|---|---|---|---|
| No. of columns | 1 | 8 | 4 | 4 | 2 | 5 | 6 | 1 |

Two records per card.

APPENDIX 5.4

SALES ORDER CARD

| Card Type | Customer No. | Consignee N/A | Cust. Order No. | Own Order No. | Carriage charge | Method of Dispatch | Pattern code | Qty | Pattern code | Qty | Pattern code | Qty |
|---|---|---|---|---|---|---|---|---|---|---|---|---|
| 1 | 8 | 28 | 6 | 6 | 4 | 1 | 6 | 2 | 6 | 2 | 6 | 2 |

No. of columns

CASH CARD

| Card Type | Customer No. | Date | Ref No. | Value |
|---|---|---|---|---|
| 1 | 8 | 6 | 6 | 7 |

No. of columns

CUSTOMER AMENDMENT CARD
118 characters = Two cards.

## APPENDIX 5.5

### FILE RECORD LAYOUT

DISC

STOCK RECORDS

| | Pattern No. | Price | Qty | Min Stk | Max Stk | Re-order Qty | Date of last movement |
|---|---|---|---|---|---|---|---|
| Number of chars | 8 | 4 | 4 | 2 | 4 | 4 | 6 |

SALES ANALYSIS RECORD

| | Area No. | Comm code | Value | Comm code | Value | Comm code | Value | Comm code | Value | Comm code | Value | Comm code |
|---|---|---|---|---|---|---|---|---|---|---|---|---|
| Number of chars | 3 | 2 | 7 | 2 | 7 | 2 | 7 | 2 | 7 | 2 | 7 | 2 |

## FILE RECORD LAYOUT

### CUSTOMER MASTER RECORD

MAGNETIC TAPE

| | No. of chars in record | Customer No. | Name and address | Area No. | Trade discount | Retail or whl | Credit limit | No. of chars invoice records | No. of chars cash records |
|---|---|---|---|---|---|---|---|---|---|
| Number of chars | 3 | 8 | 100 | 3 | 1 | 1 | 5 | 2 | 2 |

Fixed length →

| | Comm 01 | Comm 02 | Comm 03 | Comm 04 | — — — — | Comm 39 | Comm 40 |
|---|---|---|---|---|---|---|---|
| Number of chars | 6 | 6 | 6 | 6 | | 6 | 6 |

Fixed length →

| | Date | Opening balance | Date | Inv No. | Value | Date | Inv No. | Value | — — — — | Date | Rec No. | Value |
|---|---|---|---|---|---|---|---|---|---|---|---|---|
| Number of chars | 6 | 7 | 6 | 6 | 6 | 6 | 6 | 6 | | 6 | 6 | 7 |

Variable length →

# APPENDIX 5.7

INVOICING, STOCK CONTROL
SALES LEDGER AND SALES STATISTICS

S/A..................      Daily      Date..................

### RUN 01

*Input*: Stock amendments-
additions, deletions, price
changes, etc.

*Update*: Stock File on disc
with amendments.

*Print:* Errors, mismatches.
List details of amendments
written to Stock File.

### RUN 02

*Input:* Three card packs
(1) customer amendments
(2) sales orders
(3) cash received in that
    order.
    Outstanding Orders File
    from previous day run
    before sales order pack
    for current day.

*Output:* Customer amendments
written to tape.
Outstanding orders and
current orders matched with
Stock File records. Stock
available—update stock
record. Extend order and
write to magnetic tape.
Stock not available—write
order to Outstanding Orders
File for input next day.
Print stock status report.

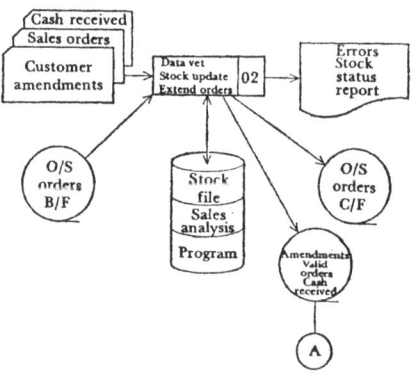

S/A.................              Daily              Date.................

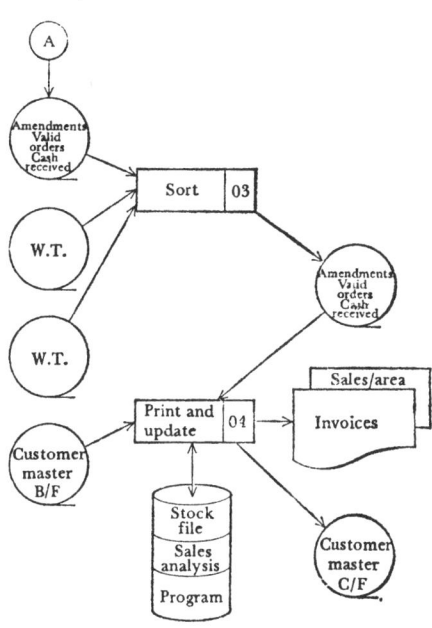

**RUN 03**

Sort to customer number
order.

**RUN 04**

*Input:* Sorted customer
amendments, valid orders,
cash received.

*Update:* Customer Master
File. Match with customer
record.

(1) update for amendments
(2) check balance of account
    plus current orders not
    in excess of credit limit.
    If in excess print 'order
    not acceptable' on invoice,
    otherwise print invoice
(3) write cash received to
    customer record
(4) update appropriate
    commodity field in
    customer record by value
    of order
(5) update commodity field
    within area record on
    disc by value of order.

*Output*

(1) updated Customer Master
    File
(2) invoices
(3) at end of run print value
    of sales by area from disc.

S/A.................       Monthly       Date.................

RUN 11

*Input:* Customer Master File.

*Update:* Customer Master File, delete invoice totals and cash received fields, calculate and write new opening balance.

*Output:* Customers' statements with sales per customer by commodity printed. Updated Customer Master File.

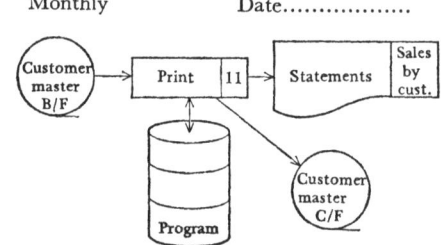

RUN 12

*Output:* Print sales by commodity within area from disc in duplicate. Copy becomes representatives' commision statement.

RUN 13

*Output:* Print sales by commodity for each area.

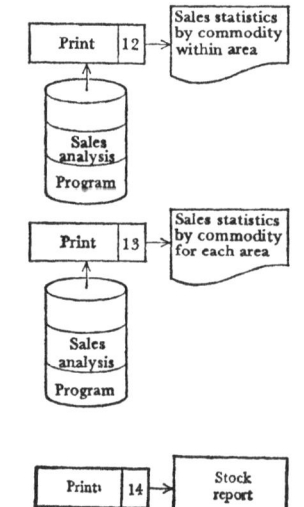

RUN 14

*Output:* Print from disc stock report. Stock at or below minimum. Stock above maximum. Date stock last moved.

# CASH COLLECTION

### GENERAL GUIDELINES

The uneven flow of work is likely to be a problem with any system. Ideally, the renewals falling due on the four quarter days would be spread evenly over the remaining days of the year, but the free cover required to achieve this would be costly. Not all the policies due in March are renewable on the quarter day, but if carried out unselectively, moving the quarter-day renewals forward by an average of forty-five days would represent a loss of premium income of more than £1 million. Even moving only those policies with a premium of £2 would cost approximately £93,000. Moving the renewal date for those policies with a premium of £2 forward only ten to twenty days at a cost of £30,000 so that they come into the next month, but adjusting the date of renewal dispatch so that renewals for quarter-month cases are sent out well before renewal date, limits the normal daily maximum to 9,000 per day, which is considered acceptable.

### GUIDELINES FOR PROBLEM 1

Among techniques which might be considered are:
1. Substituting an accounting machine for the handwritten cash book.
2. Centralising or regionalising the procedures.
3. Encouraging payment through banks by accepting responsibility for any bank Giro charge.
4. Semi-computerising by providing a file of interpreted punch cards which would be pulled as payments were made. This method is rendered less attractive by the high proportion of changed payments.

Weekends and holiday periods will cause significant fluctuations whatever action is taken, and there is therefore no justification in carrying the spreading procedure to the ultimate.

### GUIDELINES FOR PROBLEM 2

(a) The following system is based on the use of an I.B.M. 1287 Optical Reader which was mentioned in the case study. This machine can read pre-printed or computer-printed figures. Handwritten figures can also be read provided certain constraints as to size and style of writing are followed.

There are a number of alternative optical readers covering a wide price range which might be suitable.

Mark sensing might also be used. Although it would probably be difficult to code all the information required by this application on a form of acceptable size, this might be overcome by using a short reference to access the full reference held on magnetic tape or a direct-access device.

In considering the use of an optical character reader, careful consideration must be given to the costs involved. The monthly rental of £1,500 is about equal to the cost of 5,000 punched and verified cards per working day, so that this reader would be difficult to cost-justify for this application above. The wide variations in daily input, coupled with the need for daily processing, would, however, make it difficult to employ an adequate number of punch operators to cover all situations. It will also be noted from the speed given that there is considerable excess capacity, and this is used for the reconciliation of credit agents' statements of account. Fortunately the two applications taken together do cost-justify the optical reader.

Fields such as the policy number, which may contain alphabetic information, are numerically coded so that they can be read on the numeric reader. One system which has been successfully used allocates a numerical value to the letters of the alphabet and assumes that the reference is a number with a base of 36. This number is then converted to the normal base of 10 for printing on a document and when optically read is converted back.

The optical reader may misread or be unable to read some characters. A check character – say modulus 10 – may enable an unreadable character to be reconstructed and will also provide a check on misreading. Alternatively, or additionally, the code line can be duplicated and both lines can be read and compared.

One possible system is described below:

1. To separate cash from other incoming post, a box number may be used if the Post Office are prepared to grant this

facility. If an envelope of a distinctive colour is enclosed, this will help with the separation.

2. Envelopes are slit open under supervision using an electric letter-opener, but contents are not removed.

3. The contents are removed, again under supervision, and all cheques and postal orders are crossed to the Group with a rubber stamp. It is important to ensure that this is carried out on every item as once crossed in this fashion the risk of theft is greatly minimised. On some days bank notes are received, but never many. Any bank notes are handed to the official in charge, entered in a book and the entry initialled by the person who removed the note from the envelope. The clerk in charge retains the cash and supplies in return a cash substitute which is a simple form stating the amount of cash it represents.

4. As the cheques are crossed they are sorted together with their accompanying counterfoils into three baskets:

(i) cheque, or postal order, with one counterfoil;

(ii) two or more remittances or two or more counterfoils;

(iii) no counterfoils, or counterfoil with accompanying letter.

5. A clerk takes the single counterfoils with single remittances and checks that the amount of the remittance and the amount shown on the counterfoil are the same. If not, the amount of the remittance is handwritten in the boxes on the counterfoil

The back of the cheque or postal order is date-stamped and numbered with an automatic numbering stamp.

6. At intervals of about fifty items batch headers are introduced (see p. 119). These are pre-printed forms which are perforated so that they form three parts. Two of the parts are put with the counterfoils, the other with the cheques. All parts have the same pre-printed number. The part put with the cheques is also stamped on the face with the automatic numbering stamp.

7. The cheques are punched, preferably on paper or magnetic tape as cards may get out of order. Only the amount of each cheque or postal order is punched, but the pre-printed number and the number added by the automatic numbering stamp is punched when a batch header is encountered. If a good punch operator is used, verification is unnecessary

because all discrepancies will be detected by the computer. Output should be between 1 and 2 key depressions per second.

8. The counterfoils and batch headers are read by the optical reader and written to disc.

One of the batch headers is always selected to the reject pocket under program control so that if any of the following counterfoils are rejected because of an unreadable character, the batch they are from can be identified.

9. Items which are rejected by the optical reader will be selected to the reject pocket, but in addition a form will be printed indicating which characters have not been read (see p. 120). By handwriting the information in boxes on the form, the unread characters can be reintroduced via the optical reader. The computer-printed form carries a batch number and sequence number so that the rejected item can be sorted back into its correct sequence by the computer. The 1287 reader does have a cathode ray tube to display unreadable characters and provision for keying rejected data directly into the reader, but the reduction in throughput which this would cause may not be acceptable.

10. Counterfoil information and cash information is sorted on the computer into sequence number within batch. The computer is then able to align on the batch headers and pair off the cash particulars with the information on the counterfoils. If an item does not pair it will be omitted for the time being, but otherwise the items will be tagged as paired.

At the end of the batch the computer will total any unpaired cash and unpaired counterfoils in the batch, and if equal will try again to pair them using various sequences of order until all have been agreed or the machine is unable to agree and is forced to print out unpaired items.

11. To help this pairing where there are two or more counterfoils or more than one cheque, a multiple-item form is inserted immediately in front of the counterfoils concerned which states the number of counterfoils and number of remittances which are to be paired (see p. 120). It was for this reason that these items were separated initially.

12. From time to time a control card will be fed into the computer instructing it to print a paying-in list. It will then

produce a list of remittances associated with agreed batches showing the number on the batch header at intervals on the list. The cheques associated with the agreed batches can be readily identified by the batch headers which are slightly larger than the cheques, and thus the batch header reference can be easily read. These cheques and lists are taken to the bank at intervals during the day. Care is taken to ensure that any bank notes, etc., received are put into a separate batch to facilitate banking. One part of the paying-in list also shows the full reference of the policy taken from the counterfoil and the sequence number deduced to be stamped on the cheque.

13. Items without counterfoils or otherwise requiring special processing were sorted at outset into a third group. Where a sufficient reference is available, a dummy counterfoil is hand-written and then punched. Mutilated counterfoils are similarly punched.

If the nature of the payment cannot be identified it is given a special dummy reference and then processed normally. A note of the dummy reference is kept with the papers until the payment can be properly identified, when it can be reversed and allocated.

14. If a cheque is returned 'R.D.', the date and serial number stamped on the back enable it to be related back to the paying-in list and thus the identification of the policy, etc., concerned can be ascertained so that the entries can be reversed.

15. Reversals of cheques and transfers to other bank accounts are advised to the computer by punched cards. At the close of each day a magnetic tape is produced of all payments received and agreed, for use in updating the main accounting file. At the same time the computer prints the brought-forward totals and amounts banked, reversed and withdrawn together with the closing balance. These figures are reconciled a few days later with the pass-book total provided by the bank.

16. There is sufficient under-utilisation of the optical reader for most machine breakdowns to be remedied and processing still completed. In the event of a prolonged failure the cheques are add-listed and banked. The normal processing is then carried out as soon as the system becomes available again.

17. A National Giro counterfoil is also provided (see p. 118). Where these are passed through the Giro system they are optically read by National Giro who supply a magnetic tape daily bearing particulars of items paid. This tape is sorted together with the output from the cash-collection system described above before updating the accounting file.

# APPENDIX 6.1

## CASH COLLECTION FLOW DIAGRAM

**MANUAL PROCEDURES**

*Cross cheques with rubber stamp*
Cheques are crossed 'A/C Payee' to reduce the risk of defalcation, and separated into three streams.

*Obtain reference and enter on slip*
A reference must be obtained or a dummy reference used to put the item on suspense. A counterfoil substitute is then handwritten.

*Check remittance agrees with total of counterfoils. Write multiple item form*
The multiple item form shows the number of cheques and number of counterfoils for those cases where an insured is paying several premiums with one cheque or is using several cheques or postal orders to pay a premium. This helps the computer program to reconcile the cheques and counterfoils.

*Cheque numbering procedure*
Cheques are examined for signature and date. They are then stamped on the back with an automatic numbering stamp which prints the date and a sequence number. Batch headers are inserted at intervals of about fifty items. The batch headers are in three parts, each bearing the same sequence number. Two parts are put with the counterfoils and one with the cheques. The part put with the cheques is also numbered in sequence with the cheques. Any counterfoils obviously unfit for optical reading are put into separate batches.

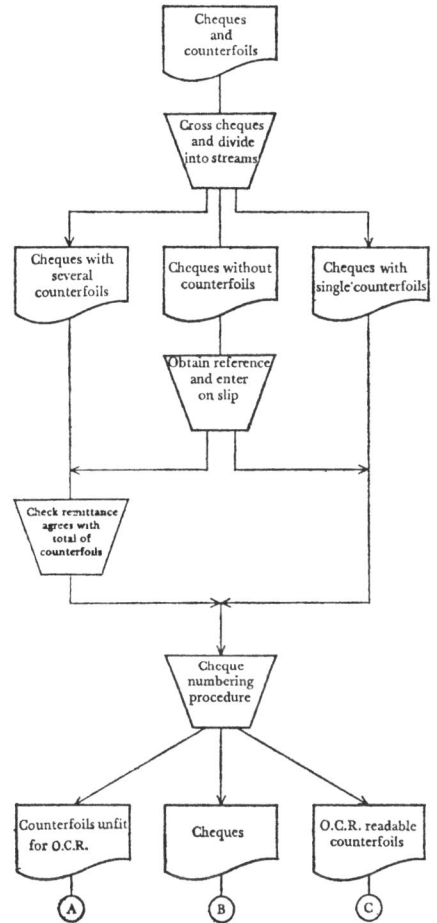

*Punching—cheques*
Punch the batch no. and
sequence no. from the batch
headers and the amount only
from the cheques.

*Punching dishonoured cheques*
Any cheques which are
returned by the bank 'R D'
must be identified using the
sequence no. and date on
the back. This allows the
stored counterfoil to be
traced and particulars are
punched and entered into
the system to set up reversing
entries.
Withdrawals from the bank
account are also punched so
that the computer maintained
total should agree with the
bank statement balance.

*Punching counterfoils unfit for OCR*
A small percentage of the total
number of counterfoils
received must be keyed.

RUN 01

*Input:* Batch headers and
cheques.
Details of payments made by
dishonoured cheques and
withdrawals.
Batch headers and counterfoils for items unsuitable for
OCR.

*Processing:* Validity check and
write out.
*Output:* Disc (or tape)—
accepted cards with batch
reference from batch header
and sequence number in
batch.
Printer—particulars of any
rejected cards.

*Cheques stored*
Cheques are stored in batch
order temporarily while
awaiting banking.

114

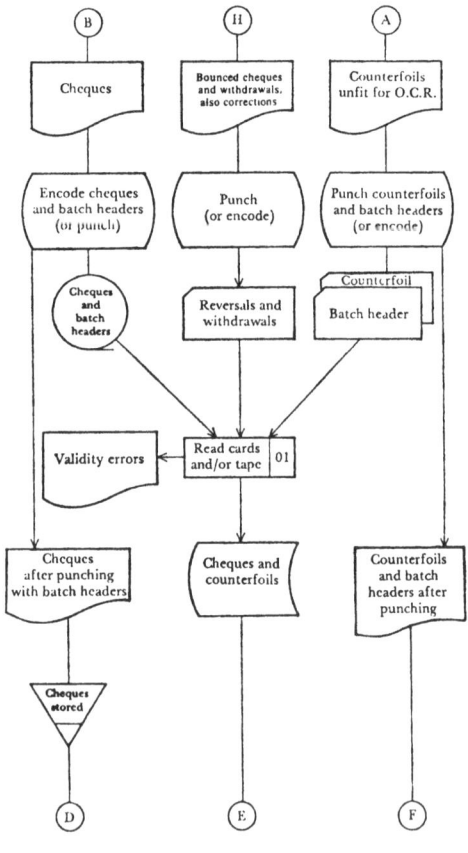

RUN 02

*Input:* Batch headers, counter-foils and multiple item forms. Correction forms.

*Processing:* Reads documents using OCR. Checks for unreadable characters and applies validity tests to detect misread characters. Part 1 of batch header is selected to first hopper with accepted documents. Part 2 of batch header is selected to second hopper with rejected documents.

*Output*
Disc (or tape)—accepted documents with batch reference from batch header and sequence in batch. Printer—correction forms showing batch and sequence number of rejected documents and all information read. Unreadable characters marked.

*Unreadable characters written on correction forms*
By reference back to the counterfoils the unread characters are obtained and entered by hand on the correction forms.
The correction forms are then read by the optical reader.

*Counterfoils stored*
The counterfoils are filed in batch order. The second part of the batch header aids the filing of the rejected counterfoils.

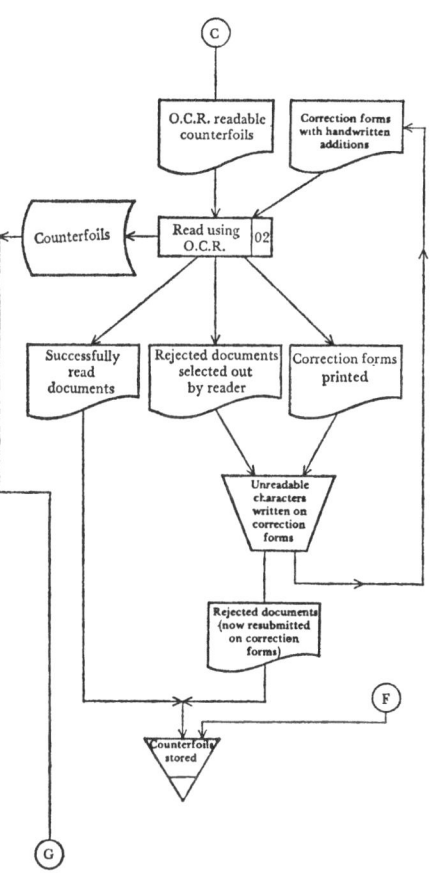

115

RUN 03

Sort to sequence within
batch within type of record.

RUN 04: *Phase 1*

The counterfoils and cheques
are written sequentially to
separate direct access data
sets. At the same time any
untagged records from the
previous run are merged with
them.

*Phase 2*
The counterfoil and cheque
files are read sequentially and
compared. When all the
cheques and counterfoils in a
batch have been reconciled
an indicator is set in the
batch header.

*Phase 3*
Agreed batches are listed to
provide paying-in list for
bank.
Disagreed batches—list
counterfoils and cheques
with disagreeing items
indicated by asterisks.

*Note:* If records are added in
many small runs a form of
indexed file organisation may
be better.

*Phase 4*
This phase is initiated at the
end of the day. The agreed
batches are written to the
Paid Items File and records
are tagged as they are written
out. Control totals obtained
by adding cheques and
subtracting reversals and
withdrawals are printed.

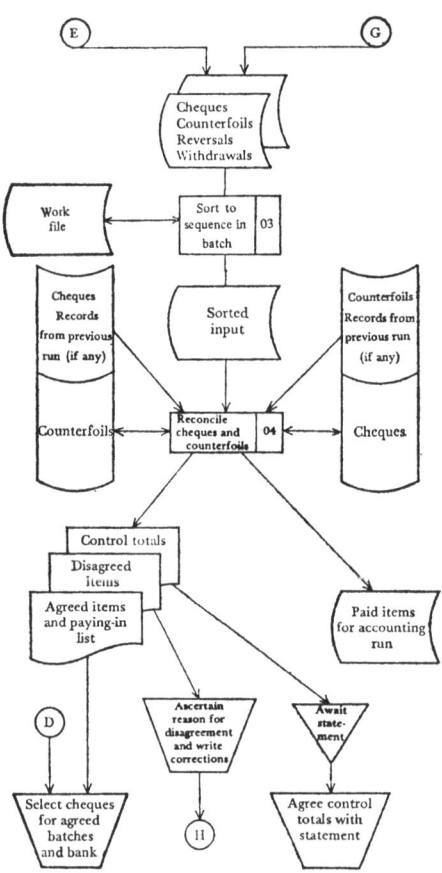

116

*Select cheques and bank*
The cheques were stored in
batch order so they can
easily be presented to the
bank in the same order as the
list.

*Disagreements and corrections*
If cheques and counterfoils
do not agree, corrections can
be input on punched cards
through Run 01.

*Agree control totals*
The bank statement totals
will be a day or two behind
the computer but they should
be compared daily.

117

# CASTLE ROCK GROUP

Head Office: London EC2

## NOTICE

The Amount stated below is due on the date shown. Please pay the amount due by one of the methods described on the back of the Payment Counterfoil. In all correspondence please quote this Policy Number.▼

Policy No. 07/ WAP0000070

Name  PETER PIPER

Cover  ALL RISKS

Due due 1.4.71   Payable within  15  days of this date

RENEWAL PREMIUM FOR 12 MONTHS

Amount Due
£251.50

### In your own interest

Is this cover adequate? If any alteration or advice is required, or if you have changed your address, please notify your agent, or our branch.

at ▶ CASTLE ROCK GROUP,
PROGRESSIVE HOUSE, 33, WELLINGTON ST.,
BRIGHTON, BN1 6HL.

Tel No.▶ 027344433

Please return this section of the notice and see note overleaf

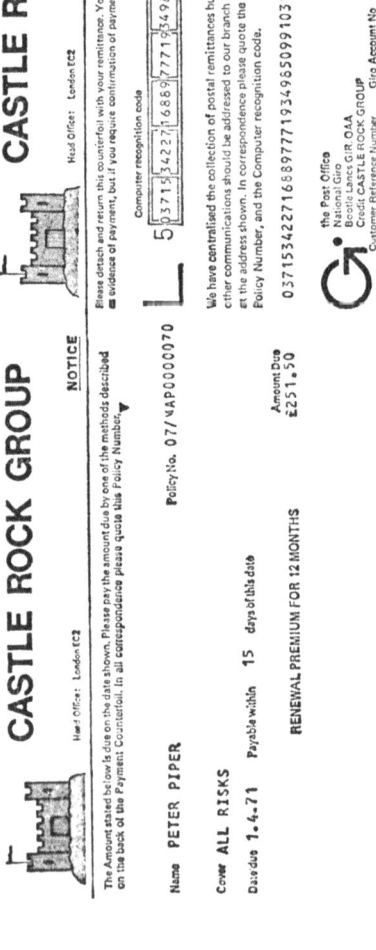

# CASTLE ROCK GROUP

Head Office: London EC2

## PAYMENT COUNTERFOIL

Please detach and return this counterfoil with your remittance. Your paid cheque will be accepted as evidence of payment, but if you require confirmation of payment please put an "X" in this box ⟶

Computer recognition code

5 93715 34227 16889 7771 94985 99910 31200 0025 150

We have centralised the collection of postal remittances but other communications should be addressed to our branch office at the address shown. In correspondence please quote the Policy Number, and the Computer recognition code.

03715342271689 77719 34985099 1031200 0025150

Date Due  1. 4.71   Serial No.   00009

the Post Office
National Giro
Bootle Lancs GIR OAA
Credit CASTLE ROCK GROUP
Customer Reference Number    Giro Account No   Amount

27A 0118   WAP0000070   446 2008   £   251.50

Branch and Agency No.   Policy No.

13 PP
2 0 8 A

PETER PIPER ESQ
21, MIDDLE HILL
HORSHAM
SUSSEX

By transfer from Giro A/no.

......................19............

Signature

The space below must be left for machine processing

AJ4L0Y1DERK14GLPWHS6X  84446200800025150X

118

F/

L I C 3 I   0 I 0 0 I 3

010013

L 2          0 I 0 0 I 3

010013

F/

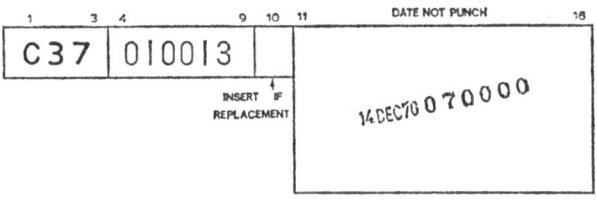

| 1 | 3 | 4 | 9 | 10 | 11 | DATE NOT PUNCH | 16 |

C37 | 0 I 0 0 I 3

INSERT   IF
REPLACEMENT

14 DEC 70 0 7 0 0 0 0

119

CENTRAL CASH COLLECTION          O.C.R. CORRECTION

COMPUTER REFERENCE

AMOUNT     RECEIPT    BATCH/SEQUENCE

└ 7

CORRECTION BOXES

H

CENTRAL CASH COLLECTION   COUNTERFOIL SUBSTITUTE   AND CASH AND COUNTERFOIL
CORRECTION ADVICE

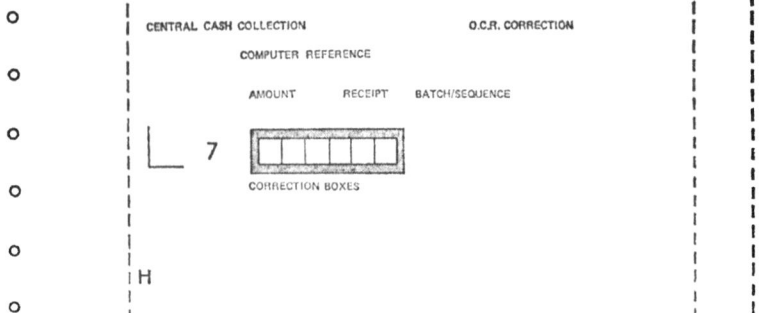

CENTRAL CASH COLLECTION             MULTIPLE ADVICE

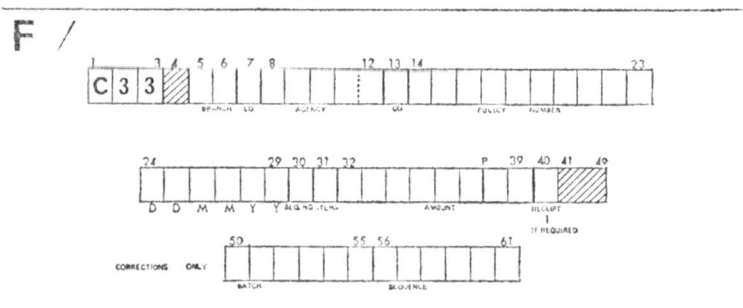

TOTAL OF CHEQUE (S)       NO. OF    NO. OF
                               CHEQUES   ADVICES

The basis for costing computer time may vary considerably.

Some organisations charge, for costing purposes, the amount for which the time could be sold on a bureau basis; others ignore the problem completely, arguing that once the computer is installed for a particular purpose other work can be added without any increase in real costs.

When more than one program is being run at the same time on a computer it is also necessary to consider how any charge is to be divided between them. This may depend upon the information which the supervisor program can provide.

It is assumed for the purposes of this example that the supervisor program records the time spent on processing in each partition, and that the charges for the central processing unit are based on a combination of the size of core used and time spent on processing.

The optical reader is slow compared with the central processing unit, and the proportion of C.P.U. time required to process the data being read is therefore quite low. This in turn results in a lower hourly charge than for some other operations such as testing where data are made available to the C.P.U. at much higher speeds from tape or disc.

The figures shown below are typical for one large organisation, but in practice the systems designer must obtain and use figures appropriate to the computer system and circumstances.

When comparing costs it is often open to argument to what extent overheads should be included. It is sometimes suggested that only direct costs should be considered because an increase or reduction in staff will not cause any increase or reduction in overhead charges. These are seldom rigidly fixed, however, and are usually subject to some variation in consequence of change.

The most satisfactory technique is possibly to cost the organisation as it would be with and without the change. If the estimates are based on the present and various dates in the future, allowance can be made for any trends in the business. It may be, for example, that a saving in staff can delay the need to move to larger accommodation. It may also be felt that wage levels will rise while machine costs are more stable.

For the purpose of the following figures the salary levels have

121

been loaded to make some allowance for overheads, but it must be kept in mind that, whilst the additional costs of the new system will almost certainly be incurred, careful control will be necessary to ensure that the savings are achieved. It is unlikely that the branch staff used for this work will be dismissed immediately the new system comes into force. It is more likely that they will be retained and redeployed as vacancies are created by natural wastage.

| *Existing Costs* | 120 staff at £2,000 | £240,000 |
|---|---|---|

*Cost of Implementing Proposed System*

| Detailed systems work, program specification, programming, systems testing | | |
|---|---|---|
| Say, 4 man-years at £4,000 | | £ 16,000 |
| Machine time for compiling and testing | | |
| 80 hours at £50 | | £ 4,000 |
| Staff training, post-implementation study, etc. | | £ 5,000 |
| | | £ 25,000 |

Any loss of premium income resulting from the redistribution of the quarter-day renewals should be added.

*Annual Costs*

| Write off implementation costs over two years | £ 12,500 |
|---|---|
| Keying cheques and unreadable documents | |
| 4 operators at £2,000 | £ 8,000 |
| Clerical staff | |
| 12 full-time at £2,000 | £ 24,000 |
| 0–24 part-time called in as input requires | £ 24,000 |
| Computer costs 750 hours at £50 | £ 37,500 |
| Rental of optical reader £18,000 | |
| say 50 per cent to this application | £ 9,000 |
| | £115,000 |

The computer costs include an element for operating and overheads.

The stationery for the central cash collection will be an insignificant factor, but if the price of the renewal notices is increased this could be significant. Special paper or special printing techniques may be required for the optical reader; if so, quotations should be obtained and this factor taken into consideration.

In addition to the cost savings there should be an increase in investment income.

Achieved reduction in cost of more than 50 per cent is, in practice, unusual for an application of this type and should be regarded with some suspicion. The existing cost of carrying out the work may be overstated and should be checked. The clerical staff requirement has been estimated on the basis of a dummy run with some mocked-up documents. Reconsideration should be given to the allowance made for exceptional conditions.

# Examination Questions

1. 'A system analyst who designs a new system and ignores the human factor, is designing a failed system.' Discuss this statement, outlining the steps you would take to overcome resistance to change and ensure the satisfactory implementation of your new system.

2. What do you understand by a check digit system? Illustrate your answer with an example of a check digit system using modulus 11.

3. Explain the terms:

   (a) sequential organisation
   (b) indexed sequential organisation
   (c) partitioned organisation

as applied to a direct-access storage device.

4. 'The future of electronic data processing lies in the development of real-time working.' Do you agree with this statement? What support would you expect from a manufacturer if you were asked to design and implement a real-time system?

5. What factors must be considered in planning for file conversion, and what alternative methods are available?

6. What advantages would you expect from the establishment of standard procedures for documentation and specification in a computer department?

7. What are the principal factors to be considered in designing a form for computer print-out?

8. Define a 'system'. What effect does an integrated computer-based system have on a business information system?

9. The transmission of data over land lines to a central computer is one of the fastest-developing techniques. What are the advantages of data transmission? What do you understand by the terms 'Simplex', 'Half Duplex', 'Duplex'?

10. For both magnetic tape and direct-access storage devices, indicate how data security is achieved and how it is possible to recommence the run after an error situation.

# Bibliography

D. H. Brandon, *Management Standards for Data Processing* (Van Nostrand, 1968).

R. Chandor, J. Graham and R. Williamson, *Practical Systems Analysis* (Hart-Davis, 1969).

D. N. Chorofas, *Selecting the Computer System* (Gee, 1967).

F. R. Crawford, *Introduction to Data Processing* (Prentice-Hall, 1968).

A. C. Donald, *Management Information Systems* (Pergamon, 1967).

R. H. Gregory and R. L. Van Horn, *Automatic Data Processing Systems* (Chatto & Windus, 1960).

J. Klein, *Working with Groups* (Hutchinson, 1961).

H. N. Laden and T. R. Gildersleeve, *System Design for Computer Application* (Wiley, 1963).

A. F. Linton, *An Introduction to Mechanised Accounts and Computers* (Pitman, 1966).

T. W. Macrae, *Impact of Computers on Accounting* (Wiley, 1964).

D. H. Saunders, *Computers in Business: An Introduction* (McGraw-Hill, 1968).

P. P. Schoderbek (ed.), *Management Systems* (Wiley, 1967).

R. Tomlin, *Managing the Introduction of Computer Systems* (McGraw-Hill, 1970).

F. G. Withington, *The Use of Computers in Business Organisations* (Addison-Wesley, 1966).